IN THE COMPANY OF
Jesus

FINDING UNCONVENTIONAL WISDOM
AND UNEXPECTED HOPE

BILL DONAHUE

InterVarsity Press
Downers Grove, Illinois

InterVarsity Press
P.O. Box 1400, Downers Grove, IL 60515-1426
World Wide Web: www.ivpress.com
E-mail: mail@ivpress.com

InterVarsity Press® *is the book-publishing division of InterVarsity Christian Fellowship/USA*®, *a student movement active on campus at hundreds of universities, colleges and schools of nursing in the United States of America, and a member movement of the International Fellowship of Evangelical Students. For information about local and regional activities, write Public Relations Dept., InterVarsity Christian Fellowship/USA, 6400 Schroeder Rd., P.O. Box 7895, Madison, WI 53707-7895, or visit the IVCF website at <www.intervarsity.org>.*

Design: Cindy Kiple

Images: bread: John T. Merkle
two fish: Kenneth Garrett/National Geographic Image Collection

ISBNs 0-8308-3275-0
978-0-8308-3275-0

Printed in the United States of America ∞

Library of Congress Cataloging-in-Publication Data

Donahue, Bill.
In the company of Jesus; finding unconventional wisdom and
unexpected hope / Bill Donahue.
p. cm.
Includes bibliographical references.
ISBN 0-8308-3275-0 (hardcover: alk. paper)
1. Jesus Christ—Person and offices. I. Title.
BT203.D66 2005
232—dc22

2005018543

P	19	18	17	16	15	14	13	12	11	10	9	8	7	6	5	4	3	2	1
Y	19	18	17	16	15	14	13	12	11	10	09	08	07	06	05				

To Gail,

whose encouragement, patience,

wisdom, discernment and unending love

make our marriage a blessing,

our family a community

and our house a home.

I love you.

CONTENTS

ACKNOWLEDGMENTS

Books are the products of teams, not authors. My team includes first and foremost a loving and amazing wife, Gail, who made sacrifices and extended grace when I burned the midnight oil. Without her prayers and encouragement, and those of my kids, Ryan and Kinsley, this book would still be stuck somewhere in my head. Thanks also to my parents and extended family—you carried me along in prayer. And how would I do life without a great group of guys who meet every Thursday morning to explore the ways and teachings of Jesus? They all inspire and motivate me.

I am also filled with gratitude for the many people at the Willow Creek Association and Willow Creek Community Church who encouraged me and provided feedback. And I am grateful for a leadership team who supported and cheered me on as I tackled this project and the Jesus 101 Bible Study Series that accompanies it. Thanks for standing with me.

I am grateful to those who read the manuscript or who gave encouragement and input from inception to publication. Much thanks to the publishing and marketing teams at Willow, and especially to Nancy Raney, Christine Anderson, Doug Yonamine and Mark Kemink for guiding this along. Thanks to Paul Prather and Kristen Aikman for their invaluable feedback and insights and perspective. And kudos to Joan Oboyski, my administrative assistant—she kept my world in order throughout the process.

Finally, I realize you would not be reading this without the very capable publishing team at IVP. They kept me focused yet remained flexible and gracious as the project evolved. The sharp insights, coaching and editing skills of Cindy Bunch and Ruth Goring kept this book from unraveling into a string of rambling thoughts and experiences. The expertise of Cindy Kiple and the design team, the efforts of the marketing team, and the leadership of Bob Fryling combined to bring this project together in a remarkable way.

Thanks to all of you. May those who read this realize that no one—especially me—ever writes alone. Doing this as a team made all the difference in the world to me.

Bill Donahue

INTRODUCTION

What images come to mind when I say "Jesus"? Religious icon, mystical guru, sandaled sage? Maybe he's the figure in the stained-glass window at church, or in the painting hanging in the hallway of your grandmother's house. Or perhaps he's the living, breathing Son of God and Son of Man who captivates us with his teaching, embraces us with his love and disarms us with his grace.

I was twenty-three years old when Jesus and faith became real to me. My journey toward God had been a bumpy one. I attended church and youth groups growing up, but I did not connect deeply with God in any real way. Some weeks I felt close to him. But most of the time, especially in college, I only dabbled in spirituality. A church service here, a campus meeting there and an occasional meaningful conversation along the way. Like many, I knew there was something about "the God thing" that was important, but over time I withdrew from formal religious activities.

I had read about Jesus, heard sermons on his life, prayed prayers "in Jesus' name" and even tried to convince a college roommate that Jesus was a historical figure. There was only one problem—I had never encountered Jesus up close and personal. Perhaps I had never taken time to get to know him, perhaps I was not ready to meet him, or maybe I was too intoxicated with myself to allow anyone into my life, especially Jesus. In any case, for years I was a distant observer, peering over the fence at him like baseball fans watching their favorite teams during spring training. Unlike those fans, though, I didn't even try to get close enough for a photo or an autograph. After all, what had I done to deserve attention from such a celebrity?

Then I encountered Jesus. And he rocked my world.

For twenty-three years I had been like Zacchaeus in the Bible, watching Jesus from the branches of a sycamore tree. And then, just like in the story, he called my name: "Bill! Bill Donahue! Come down here. I want to hang out with you today!" I leapt from the tree and began a journey in the company of Jesus and those who follow his ways.

Along the way I have discovered that you do not have just one encounter with Jesus. Each time you meet him the encounter is fresh and engaging. It adds texture and color to the relationship. You are unnerved by what he says, startled by what he does and confused by who he seems to be. On some occasions you feel you have much in common with this man from Galilee, yet moments later you are overwhelmed by his greatness and feel grateful to simply stand in the shadow of his robe.

However you view Jesus, he is certainly the most controversial figure ever to enter human history. More has been written about his life and more songs sung about him than about any other figure. Most people, especially in America, know something about Jesus—from a Sunday school teacher, a movie, a friend, a family member. But relatively few of us have ever encountered him. When we do, our image of him changes.

Have you ever seen a man speaking from a platform, stylishly dressed, articulate and professional, holding an audience in the palm of his hand? Then three days later you see that same man at a grocery store wearing a sweatsuit, chugging down a power drink after a long jog. You hardly recognize him. You first encountered him larger than life, an important and admirable figure hovering above the lives of ordinary people. Now at the checkout counter, with perspiration dripping from his forehead, he's just Bob—a regular guy like you and me.

I remember growing up watching Jimmy Stewart in movies like *It's a Wonderful Life* and thinking, *Wow, what an amazing actor!* A few years later I attended Princeton University, about forty years after Stewart himself was there. Every spring, alumni would return and parade through town and across campus. Each class wore a costume incorporating the school's colors—orange and black—and images of our tiger mascot. The older the alumni, the more conservative their costumes (though it's difficult to look distinguished wearing orange and black). The year that Jimmy Stewart returned to march with his class, the crowds were larger as the town turned out for a look at this impressive celebrity.

There he was, looking much like the rest of his classmates. A gray-haired man in his sixties, no Hollywood makeup or special lighting, wearing an orange-and-black-checkered blazer and a pair of khakis. There was something disarmingly simple and warm about him. He laughed and smiled, waved to onlookers and chatted with friends. No fanfare or pretense—he was just a normal guy. Suddenly I had a different view of Jimmy Stewart. This was a different person than I had seen on the silver screen. Oh, there was still something magical about his presence, but now he seemed like a real person, a flesh-and-blood human being. This encounter added texture and meaning to a personality I had long admired.

Many people think they know Jesus. Some admire him; some turn away at the mere mention of his name. But few have truly taken the time to sit in his company and bask in his presence. When they do, everything changes. Suddenly they are riveted by his words and overwhelmed by his actions. Whether they embrace him or reject him, all are affected by him.

This book is not a history of Jesus or a theological treatise on his roles as Prophet, Priest and King. It is not even an explanation of his various titles—Master, Lord, Savior, Creator. So much has been written in these areas that I doubt whether I could add anything of substance.

My purpose is to reveal Jesus as we encounter him in the stories of the Bible—on walks, at dinner, in the marketplace, on a hillside. I never cease to be amazed at these encounters, these moments in the company of Jesus and in the company of those who follow him. But I would like to take us further—beyond the text. It is one thing to study Jesus and pray to him and worship him. It is another to simply be with him in the context of his life and work. And that is where I'd like to take us—into the company of Jesus where we can engage him in the moment. We will meet him as teacher and friend, as lover and forgiver. We will encounter him as leader and conqueror, as healer and revealer.

As I spend time in the company of Jesus I find myself confronted with his words and inspired by his actions. I think you will also. And these encounters will create a longing to know Jesus better, to move beyond first impressions toward deeper relationship and understanding. The material in this book is a starting point on the journey to an endless stream of conversations and moments with the Son of God.

Each time I cross paths with Jesus in my life or across the pages of the Gospels or at work in others, I am called to respond. I feel compelled to answer the question, "What shall I do with Jesus?" Religious elites and political leaders of his day would have answered that question one way. Eager followers could have answered yet another. And the marginalized members of society—the weak, powerless and broken—still another. But the real question for each of us today is, "What will *we* do with Jesus?"

The question is as viable for the committed Christ-follower as it is for the spiritual seeker or the unimpressionable cynic. How do I respond to this unique person in history? Much of our response depends on where and how our path crosses his.

To help you along the journey and to maximize your interactions with this unique person, the book is structured to encourage daily readings. It is designed to promote deeper engagement and reflection. At the end of each section there will be an opportunity to process what you have just read. Three prompts will guide you here: "Personal Response," "Dialogue with God" and "Further Bible Reading."

In the "Personal Response" portion you will find a few provocative questions to chew on. This section is ideal for personal reflection and journal writing. I find it important to ask myself some hard or probing questions about what I am learning in my relationship with God, particularly with Jesus. This will start you down that path.

Next you will find a brief paragraph called "Dialogue with God." These prayers reflect some of what I feel (or have felt) in my relationship with Jesus based on how I have encountered him. They are designed to be personal—prayers you might find yourself praying. I do not intend to pray in your place or assume your thoughts. But I believe these words reflect the ideas and emotions we all experience as we encounter Jesus. Some will sound like the thoughts of a skeptic and others will reflect a deeper faith; all are expressions of real anger, joy, sadness, hope and sometimes plain confusion. For some of you, these prayers will be a starting point for further dialogue with God. Others among you may find them difficult or new. Take a risk and try praying them yourself, or put them into your own words.

Below the "Dialogue with God" prayer you'll see a suggestion for further Bible reading. If the verses used in a particular section create a hunger to know more about Jesus and his ways, then this reading will help. Most are Gospel passages from the life of Christ; a few come from other places in the Bible.

For those of you in small groups, another way to experience God while reading this book is to use the companion Jesus 101 study guides. Each kind of encounter with Jesus (as provocative teacher, sacred friend and so on) is expanded on in a study guide designed for a more engaging small group format. You can read a section of the book and then delve more deeply into the study guide. The eight study guides parallel the eight chapters of this book, and each guide is divided into six sessions of small group material. The guides can be used separately or in conjunction with *In the Company of Jesus,* whatever best serves your group.

So, what comes to mind when I say "Jesus"? Your answer to that question at the end of this book will be much different than it is now. At least that is my hope. Join me in a journey through these pages, a chronicle of small but often profound encounters with the God-Man, the most amazing, disarming and sometimes controversial person ever to breathe our air or walk our roads.

Come. Let's spend some time in the company of Jesus.

Jesus

THE PROVOCATIVE TEACHER

❧

Ever notice how certain people seem to fill a room with their presence? They simply walk in and every eye turns their way. Sometimes this magnetism is due to an individual's athletic prowess or stunning appearance. For others, it's their ability to produce astounding wealth.

Growing up, Bill Gates was probably ignored in most settings—but not today. When Gates appears on the scene, people notice. *Money* magazine in May 2002 revealed that the Microsoft titan had amassed a fortune in cash: forty billion dollars, to be exact. To help us get a handle on that sum, *Money* explains that it's enough buying power to acquire Ford, Exxon, Mobil and Wal-Mart combined. Enough to purchase four space shuttles or to write a check for the entire U.S. airline industry—twice! Or he could use the money to buy every professional football, basketball, baseball and hockey team in America. Love him or hate him, Gates is a jaw-dropper because of his financial achievements.

Long before Michael Jordan amassed a financial empire on endorsements and advertisements, he was wowing audiences with his aerial acrobatics. My son still has a poster of His Airness above his desk. In the photo, Jordan is suspended in midair, hanging precariously between the foul line and the basket. He hovers with his eyes at rim level, arm stretched above his head gripping a basketball at the moment before he slams it through the net. In the background, the audience is transfixed, sharing one expression—awe. Hundreds of mouths hang open as MJ performs his superhuman display.

Sometimes sheer physical size draws attention. When we wanted a good laugh as kids, my friends and I would watch professional wrestling. Thirty years ago it hadn't achieved the near-X-rated status it boasts today; it was just plain dumb. We laughed hysterically at characters like George "the Animal" Steele, who slobbered and drooled in front of the camera, and Toro Tanaka, whose pregame ritual included throwing salt around the ring—salt he would later rub into the eyes of his unsuspecting victim.

We snickered at most of this charade, eagerly devouring bags of potato chips and sloshing down cans of pop. But suddenly we became silent, and our sneers gave way to expressions of wonder. There he was, and he was unbelievable.

His name was Andre the Giant, a seven-and-a-half-foot, 450-pound humanoid stuffed into a pair of wrestling tights. Each pant leg was the size of a sleeping bag. His head was as big as a microwave oven. This was the closet thing to Goliath we had ever seen. A sports magazine picture of this behemoth showed his hand cupped around a cola can—a can visible only through the cracks between his fingers.

Soon the fun would begin. A hapless wannabe would enter the arena to challenge the giant, and after just a few moments, Andre would toss him around like a rag doll. The crowd was divided—and so was our fan club. Half wanted Andre to win; half cheered for the smaller David. But regardless of whose side we took, it was never boring when Andre was in the ring.

The list could go on—star athletes, business tycoons, entertainment divas, rock superstars. These are the people whose first names are part of our everyday vocabulary—Arnold, Oprah, "the Donald." And love them or hate them, we can't simply ignore them. They don't get lost in the crowd; no one yawns when they enter the room.

ENCOUNTERING THE PROVOCATIVE TEACHER

Despite all the fanfare generated by famous stars and athletes, no one ever caused jaws to drop like Jesus. And no one ever divided a room more quickly than this prophet from Nazareth. It was not his wealth or size or physical ability that people noticed; he didn't even have a permanent home. Certainly "he had no beauty or majesty to attract us to him / nothing in his appearance that we should desire him" (Isaiah 53:2). His redemptive power and grace, his authoritative teaching and nature-defying miracles, his unceasing love and abounding courage, turned heads and stirred deep emotions. His presence was unmistakable. People either loved him or hated him—but they never ignored him.

And neither can you.

Many people have read Jesus' biographies in the Gospel accounts of the Bible, and they are particularly enamored with his teaching. If Jesus was anything, he was a provocative teacher. Some have tried to discount his claims and soften the raspy edge of his unnerving and passionate remarks. But it cannot be done without warping his message and ruining the picture of his true character.

"Much of the history of Christianity has been devoted to domesticating Jesus," says Andrew Greeley, "to reducing that elusive, enigmatic, paradoxical person to dimensions we can comprehend, understand and convert to our own purposes. So far it hasn't worked." I couldn't agree more. Regarding Jesus' sayings, Greeley comments that they all "seem vague, slippery, disturbing and dangerous. Jesus is as disturbing now as he was in his own time: as troublesome, as much a threat to the public order." Disturbing, provocative, enigmatic.

Not exactly the Jesus many of us grew up with, the cute Jesus frolicking among the sheep and handing out goodies to his kids like grandma with a jar of homemade Christmas cookies.

Don Everts, in his compelling and earthy book *Jesus with Dirty Feet,* describes the utterly unique presence and impact of Jesus as he bounded across the stage of world history in the first century A.D.

> He was nothing like anyone had ever seen. There was something so clear and beautiful and true and unique and powerful about Jesus that old rabbis would marvel at his teaching, young children would run and sit in his lap, ashamed prostitutes would find themselves weeping at his feet, whole villages would gather to hear him speak, experts in the law would find themselves speechless, and people from the poor to the rugged working class to the unbelievably wealthy would leave everything . . . to follow him.

Jesus' teaching was . . . provocative.

Provocative. The English word has its roots in the Latin *prōvocāre,* which means "to call forth." To call forth action, response, thought. Similar in scope is the word *educate,* from *ēducāre,* which means "to lead out." If we could describe Jesus' teaching with terms like these, we might say he was "leading his students out"—out of timidity, complacency, falsehood and self-absorption—and "calling them forth" to action. Jesus called followers to experience a new way of life in the kingdom of God: a life of love, community and wholeness.

With Christ as his model, Parker Palmer has argued, "To teach is to create a space where obedience to truth can be practiced." Obedience is simply the process of aligning oneself with God's reality. The word literally means "to listen from below," implying a humility toward learning. Jesus, we might say, was a master at creating learning environments (spaces) in which truth was revealed so that it could be encountered, processed and practiced—in a word, obeyed. It was never Jesus' intent to simply comfort or entertain his students. His Sunday sermons never left hearers saying, "Nice talk; I like the way Jesus told that story about the shepherd boy and the little sheep. Of course, his message did run a bit long this week."

Not a chance. When Jesus was speaking, the room split into two groups—those who longed to hear him again, and those who wanted to run him out of town. His message portrayed a ruddy realism, the kind that fishermen and tax collectors and centurions could understand. Inspiring . . . convicting . . . provocative.

> When Jesus had finished saying these things, the crowds were amazed at his teaching, because he taught as one who had authority, and not as their teachers of the law. (Matthew 7:28-29)

> Thus the people were divided because of Jesus. (John 7:43)

Let's look closely at this provocative teacher, this disturbing and heart-rending communicator. But first, a caution. It can be tempting to simply dissect Jesus' words, much like the religious and political elite of his day. Of course, it's okay to begin there, to pick his teaching apart, slice his words into pieces with our exegetical scalpels and scrutinize them under a literary microscope. But if we stop there we fall prey to an old trap—gathering knowledge to satisfy our curiosity or, worse, harnessing information to be used as a sword for intellectual jousting matches with friends or critics. We may win the war of words or congratulate ourselves on our ability to think deeply, but in reality, we lose either way. We will find ourselves forever parsing the message yet never encountering the messenger. I have been there—and it is a cold, stale place to be.

In a New Testament class in seminary, we were studying 1 Corinthians 13, the "love chapter." The substitute professor that day was caught off-guard by a question, and soon we were off on a rabbit trail, miles away from the point of the passage. "What are the tongues of angels, and what do they sound like?" the student asked, referring to verse 1. For forty minutes students offered a variety of possibilities based on their personal study of the text. There were seven scholarly views on the subject, if I recall correctly, and we debated every one of them. I found myself sucked into the controversy. When the class ended, the irony struck me. How foolish. No one knows what the tongue of an angel sounds like. That's not the point. 1 Corinthians 13 is about love. Yet I and others had become clanging cymbals, each of us clamoring to prove our point while ignoring the love we had been called to embrace. We overlooked love, and never encountered the Lover.

So I have a challenge for you. Try to approach Jesus' teaching by reaching beyond the purely analytical toward the conversational and even the transformational. Ignore the minutiae. Courageously ask, "What is my response to this? How do I react when Jesus teaches this way? What questions do I have for him? How does this teaching provoke me to action, anger, sadness, frustration or perhaps awe? Do I find myself moving toward Jesus, or turning away? In either instance, why?"

If you authentically engage in dialogue with his story and his words, I suspect you will find yourself encountering the real Jesus. After all, he didn't just bring a message—he became the message. Or as Eugene Peterson translates it, "The Word became flesh and blood, / and moved into the neighborhood" (John 1:14 *The Message*).   .

As you read the stories of Jesus in the Bible, be aware that a few jaw-dropping experiences may lie ahead. Don't try to prepare for them; it will spoil the adventure. Just be present, available and attentive. In certain moments, perhaps when you least expect it, his words will leap off the page, prodding and provoking, calling you to act or to choose. "He who has an ear, let him hear" (Revelation 13:9).

THE TEACHER WHO SHATTERS OUR ILLUSIONS

You have heard that it was said . . . But I say . . . (NRSV)

One of my favorite teachers once proclaimed, "What we need is more disillusioned people in this world." Hardly the words one would expect from a seasoned veteran of the classroom. Perhaps we need more responsible people. Or more intelligent people. Certainly more people who vote and pay taxes. But more disillusioned people? Hmmm, maybe this professor was moonlighting as a psychotherapist and needed clients.

But as he elaborated on his comment I knew he was right. We live in a world filled with illusions—some are physical, some mental, others spiritual. Thanks to advances in cosmetic surgery, for instance, if we don't like what we see we can hide it, stretch it, tighten it, tuck it, remove it, enhance it and replace it—all in the same day. We can gently spoon-feed our illusions to ourselves or indulge in full-fledged fantasies of unending health, limitless prosperity and eternal beauty, avoiding the inner poverty and despair that often map our souls.

Illusions allow us to erect a safe and comfortable façade. And if we cannot fund our masquerade with existing financial resources, we can maintain the hoax by borrowing money we don't have to buy stuff we don't need to impress people we don't know. And on it goes. Unfortunately, like a silk burial shroud, these skin-level accouterments only provide a glamorous covering for a decaying interior. Our cosmetic and monetary enhancements are vain attempts to flee the real truth about life and death, about weakness and insecurity.

The Pharisees in Jesus' day needed a strong dose of disillusionment. They viewed themselves as righteous and pure, their perfectionist noses high above the riffraff that made up the multitudes around them. But when they encountered Jesus, he took aim at their false piety and began shattering their self-righteous illusions.

> Woe to you [Pharisees], because you are like unmarked graves, which men walk over without knowing it. (Luke 11:44)

When it comes to illusions, Jesus is on a search-and-destroy mission. His teaching rips away the surface garments, exposing the real fabric beneath.

Three little words. Jesus' most popular itinerant message, the Sermon on the Mount, was designed to destroy the self-righteous "at least I'm better than the next guy" attitude that prevailed in his day. The Pharisees may have embodied this mindset, but everyone shared in the charade. Each time Jesus spoke the words, "You have heard that it was said," people in the crowd began to nod in agreement. *You tell 'em Jesus! Let those sinners have it. Tell it like it is! Lay down the law. No holds barred; no punches pulled. Wow, this is my kind of teacher!*

But as soon as they began celebrating their sin-management strategies—having avoided any really *big* blunders like murder or adultery—Jesus rocked their worlds with three simple but arresting words: "But I say . . ." (NRSV).

Three disturbing words; three unnerving words. "But I say . . ."

These three words meant "Pay attention! What's coming next will leave your head spinning and your heart trembling. I'm about to turn your world upside down and give you a reality check."

Read Matthew 5—7 and you will discover that part of Jesus' sermon contains a string of unrelenting exposés that leave his audience either stunned and confused or seething with anger. Here are a few provocative statements from Matthew 5 that landed on the listening crowd.

> You have heard that it was said to those of ancient times, "You shall not murder."
>
> *But I say* to you that if you are angry with a brother or sister, you will be liable to judgment.
>
> You have heard that it was said, "You shall not commit adultery."
>
> *But I say* to you that everyone who looks at a woman with lust has already committed adultery with her in his heart.
>
> You have heard that it was said, "An eye for an eye and a tooth for a tooth."
>
> *But I say* to you, Do not resist an evildoer.
>
> You have heard that it was said, "You shall love your neighbor and hate your enemy."
>
> *But I say* to you, Love your enemies and pray for those who persecute you. (NRSV, emphasis added)

Each time the provocative teacher speaks, the structures of conventional wisdom that protect our illusions come crashing to the ground. It should not surprise us. In that day his words separated friends, split families and shocked followers. Every time he taught he was sparring with prevailing opinion. If a man takes your jacket from you—give him your shirt as well, he says. If someone strikes you on the cheek, turn the other toward him. Love your enemies; bless those who persecute you. Lend to those who cannot pay you back.

I remember encountering these statements for the first time and thinking that they were powerful words—poignant, clear and amazingly simple. But quickly my emotions caught up with my analysis. I wondered if these attitudes could really work in this world, or whether Jesus was even remotely in touch with reality. I found myself asking, "Is Jesus aware that my coworker is taking credit for my ideas? Does this first-century rabbi realize that throwing money to people who can't pay it back displays not only poor business judgment but exposes people to financial suicide? And what kind of defense policy would our nation have if we took cheek-turning seriously?"

But there I stood—face to face with Jesus and his teaching. No answers came. No easy way to reconcile these commands with my logic. His unsettling words pounded at my preconceived notions of reality like the ocean waves that relentlessly battered the New Jersey shoreline I frequented as a youth. And I kept mulling over those three little words—words that ambushed a hillside crowd two thousand years ago, words that still challenge the spiritual status quo.

"You have heard that it was said . . . but I say . . ."

When I encounter Jesus' teaching, I find my illusions shattering like glass on a tile floor. Here are some of them:

If I follow God, he will keep me healthy.

My kids will grow up loving God because we pray with them every night.

If I love my neighbor, she will respond in friendship.

God helps those who help themselves.

Christians deserve a better place in life.

If I study hard and get good grades, colleges will beg me to apply.

If God wants us to move, he will help us sell our home quickly.

I can manage my greed and lust on my own.

After all I have done for God, he should give me a little slack.

I hate to admit thoughts like these. And I would die wallowing in them if I had never encountered the provocative teacher who cared enough to smash my self-centered illusions in order to show me a deeper reality. One that draws me to depend on his mercy and long for his grace.

As we encounter Jesus, the provocative and unsettling teacher, we have a choice. When his words agitate our emotions or prompt deep reflection, how do we respond? It would be easy to walk away, or to think, *Okay, I'm not perfect. Nobody is. Can we move on with life?* But if we allow the process to take root, we can pursue the kind of kingdom life Jesus is calling forth in us. The kind he is provoking. We can allow our illusions of truth and reality to crumble before us, giving way to a new way of thinking. In doing so, we might see God begin to act in amazing ways in our lives, and in the world around us.

PERSONAL RESPONSE

Examine your heart right now. Does the thought of having your illusions shattered produce fear or freedom? It's risky business. He might stand your world on end.

❧ DIALOGUE WITH GOD

God, I am often unnerved by Jesus' teaching. It startles me and I feel un-easy. My soul becomes unsettled, yet I admit that certain desires emerge. Desires to discover deeper truth about you and about me. I know you are trying to break through. If you must shatter some illusions along the way, have at it. I am listening. I am ready to be taught. But you might find me a difficult student at times. So help me overcome my petty insecurities and preoccupations with my version of reality, and let me see the real world and the real Jesus. That is what I ask today.

❧ FURTHER BIBLE READING

Matthew 5—7

THE TEACHER WHO RENEWS OUR MINDS

He told them many things in parables.

Great teachers not only dispel myths and shatter illusions, great teachers make you think. Whether you want to or not.

My seventh-grade science instructor was well liked. After all, science class is a junior high boy's dream—minor chemical explosions to watch, frogs to dismember, and field trips to swamps and museums to take. Everything we loved—and everything our moms tried to keep us from—was in that science room. It was a veritable wonderland, furnished with scalpels, scissors, ropes, electrical wires, oil, glue and dead amphibians soaking in formaldehyde. Now there's a smell that camps out in the nostrils for life.

One day our teacher calmly entered the room, walked past a dozing student and placed a glass beaker on a desk in the center of the room. The beaker was half filled with water. For a moment he stared at the beaker. Then he gave us a set of simple instructions.

"Take out your journals," he said. "Turn to a blank page and then, in groups of four, record seventy-five observations of this." He pointed to the beaker.

We looked at each other for a moment. Teachers relish these moments, when students aren't sure whether they're being toyed with or whether this will be on the final exam. The silence was broken when a brazen student—try to guess his name—offered the first observation. "Okay, here's one. I see a glass of water sitting on the table." A ripple of chuckles moved across the room. Chalk one up for the students!

"Nice try, Mr. Donahue, but you have misunderstood the assignment. That was an interpretation, not an observation."

As the laughter subsided, he continued, "Observations would sound something like this: 'There is a small cylindrical object sitting on a flat surface. The object appears to contain a clear liquid.' And so on."

Now gripped by the gravity of the task before us, we began to calculate how much mental effort would be required to generate seventy-five of these statements. A collective sigh filled the room.

"You may begin," the teacher said. "We'll stop in forty minutes." He sat down at his desk as my group began struggling to fill our first page.

Mercifully, after what seemed like forty days, the bell rang and we closed our journals. "Well, I hope you got off to a good start," the teacher said. A good *start?* "Tomorrow when you come in, you can continue the work by making another seventy-five observations."

So much for wonderland. By the end of the second day, one student had recorded 225 observations, and we plotted his demise, thinking of creative ways to use the ever-pungent formaldehyde. But the smell deterred us. So did the prospect of twenty years in jail.

I learned something in those two days. Observations come to

those who ask. And the person who asks the most questions wins. Whether we liked it or not, our teacher was training us to think like scientists—to ask, to observe, to record our findings. He wanted us to observe phenomena before interpreting what we saw—or thought we saw. (Was it really water, or was it liquid nitrogen? Was the beaker glass or plastic?) He knew that we students saw what we were conditioned to see, making rash judgments before taking in the data, and he wanted to change those habits. So does Jesus.

Our minds operate according to a set of assumptions that influence how we observe and interpret truth. In order for our minds to think clearly, they must be cleansed and refreshed—renewed—so that we can receive deeper, transforming truth. So that we can look beyond snap judgments and surface observations.

Jesus was a master at mind renewal. He knew that the mind was the portal through which we process and apply truth. But truth is accessible only to the receptive mind. The student must be willing to learn. Truth can't be stuffed into the brain like the fifteenth pair of socks in a drawer that holds ten. An old Chinese proverb states, "When the student is ready, the teacher appears." But how do we know if we really want to learn? Are we ready for the mysteries of the kingdom? Can we handle the whole truth? Like youngsters learning to read, when will we be done with picture books and ready for volumes of prose and poetry, imagination and reflection?

Parables functioned as mind-renewing tools in the teaching repertoire of Jesus. His artful weaving of truth and story, of reality and simplicity, silenced foes and stunned seekers. He used parabolic lessons to make people think differently about God's kingdom and to test their receptivity to kingdom perspectives.

The kingdom of heaven is like yeast that a woman took and

mixed into a large amount of flour until it worked all through the dough. . . .

The kingdom of heaven is like treasure hidden in a field. When a man found it, he hid it again, and then in his joy went and sold all he had and bought that field.

Again, the kingdom of heaven is like a merchant looking for fine pearls. When he found one of great value, he went away and sold everything he had and bought it. (Matthew 13:33, 44-46)

These sayings brought light to the eyes of seekers but cast a veil of darkness over critics and cynics, hiding the truth under a shroud of mystery. Their minds became dull because their hearts had become hard. As a result they saw only "a glass of water sitting on a table." They missed the opportunity to look beyond the obvious.

This is why I speak to them in parables:

"Though seeing, they do not see;
　　though hearing, they do not hear or understand. . . .
For this people's heart has become calloused;
　　they hardly hear with their ears,
　　and they have closed their eyes.
Otherwise they might see with their eyes,
　　hear with their ears,
　　understand with their hearts
and turn, and I would heal them." (Matthew 13:13-15)

Understand . . . turn . . . and be healed. Amazing. Spiritual healing comes to those who allow their hearts to be renewed so that they understand, and who turn from misguided perceptions in the process of repentance. So first I ask myself, *Am I ready for such a turn? Is my mind prepared to pierce through the layers of confusion, doubt and cyni-*

cism that cloud my spiritual senses? These are tough questions for each of us. How do we answer them?

There is only one way to find out. Take the parable test. Read the sayings of the always-provoking, ever-disturbing teacher. Is the hidden truth breaking through? If so, will you allow it to shape your thoughts and renew your mind? If the truth does not crystallize before your eyes and remains difficult to find, all is not lost—unless you give up the search. In Jesus' parables, treasure hunters become treasure finders. The seeker is rewarded; the critic goes home empty-handed (or empty-headed, as the case may be). So remember, the one who asks the most questions wins.

PERSONAL RESPONSE

Why is it difficult to see things as Jesus describes? His world seems to run on an entirely different operating system, and our hardware is not compatible with his software. Think—really think—for a moment. What would it take for our hearts and minds to synchronize with that of Jesus?

DIALOGUE WITH GOD

Oh God, sometimes your message is hard to understand and even harder to follow. Other times it flows freely into my mind, changing the way I see my world, my soul and my relationship to you. Open the eyes of my heart, I ask today. Renew my mind.

This is dangerous, but I want to take a risk. I am praying a bold prayer. Move me from cynic to skeptic and from skeptic to spiritual seeker. I have a thirst for truth and knowledge about you—and if that leads me to a deeper knowledge of you, then take me there. I am eager to have my mind renewed. Go ahead. Please let me see what I cannot now, so that I can become what I cannot be without you. That is what I ask today.

❧ FURTHER BIBLE READING

Matthew 13:1-43

THE TEACHER WHO EXPOSES OUR MOTIVES

Knowing their thoughts, Jesus said . . .

We all like to think we have the best intentions when we deal with relationships. As Jean Vanier says, "While we are alone, we could believe we loved everyone." Indeed. Our self-deception often runs deep when it comes to motives.

I was part of a small group in which one of our members described a desperate situation and appealed to the group for help. A man had run out on his wife, leaving the woman, three children and no income behind. He wondered if we could take care of some of her needs while she found a job and got back on her feet. Some of us decided to mow her lawn that summer. One very hot and humid day I was sweating behind the mower when this running dialogue began in my head.

"Where is the woman who lives here? Every time we come, she's not home."

Why do you need to know?

"Because I'd just like to see her. I've never met her."

But why do you need to see her?

Then Jesus revealed my motives.

"Because I want to be thanked."

Why do you need to be thanked? Can't you serve her in secret as I have taught you?

I remember feeling embarrassed, but suddenly I realized God was changing me in that moment. What were my real motives for helping people? Did I need recognition, money, a gift or a "thank you"? Was it not enough to simply serve this needy person? Those questions—questions about my real motives—sent me on an inward journey. I had to get at the root of this need for recognition. That encounter with Jesus behind a lawnmower on a hot summer day began to transform me, and I am still growing as a result of it.

We are all capable of motives that are less than pure. Sure, there are a few moments when we shine, when the other guy is more important and self-promotion takes a back seat to self-denial. But too often, the only guy we really care about greets us every morning in the mirror. Whether we are naive about our own darkness or we cunningly manipulate the system to our own ends, self-preservation is the supreme objective. More often than not, it's all about us.

One day Jesus' closest followers were engaged in a lively debate while walking with him to Capernaum, a city on the northwest shore of the Sea of Galilee. Just days earlier two amazing events had transpired. First, Jesus had taken Peter, James and John, his three closest disciples, to a mountain where he was supernaturally transfigured in their midst as Moses and Elijah, fresh from their heavenly domain, stood alongside. Talk about an encounter! But despite the miraculous appearance of these Old Testament heroes, God the Father spoke in no uncertain terms about who was the center of attention: "This is my Son, listen to him!" Lesson number one: Jesus is the greatest prophet, teacher and hero—he is the chosen Son of God. Any questions? Good.

Now the second event. After coming down from the mountain, Jesus had encountered a mute boy who was suffering endless torment at the hands of a relentless and sinister spirit. Fits and seizures marked his waking moments, causing him to thrash about wildly or fall into a rigid, corpselike stupor. At the words of Jesus, the spirit fled and the boy became whole and alert, fully healed. The disciples were dumbfounded. Just moments earlier they had tried but failed to eradicate this same spirit. "This kind can come out only by prayer," counseled Jesus (Mark 9:29). You cannot win spiritual battles with physical resources. Again, the attention is on Jesus.

Lesson two: Jesus has power and authority over the forces of evil. Any questions? Good.

After these two remarkable events, what topic might the disciples have been discussing as they walked to Capernaum?

Despite what they had just witnessed, the disciples were bickering with each other, asking, "Who among us is the greatest?" In other words, "Who will get the best seats at the table when Jesus sets up his government? Who's at the top of the Jesus-follower food chain?" It must have been quite a discussion. I wonder if it went something like this:

JUDAS: Jesus trusts me with the money purse, so it's clear I'm the greatest.

JAMES: No, it's me, because Jesus called me a "son of thunder."

PETER: He only calls you that because you snore so loud! You're both wrong; I'm the greatest. Jesus called me "the rock" and said I would lead his church some day.

JOHN: Yeah—then ten minutes later he called you "Satan" and said, "Get behind me." Get a grip on reality, Peter.

BARTHOLOMEW: Does anyone have an extra bagel?

Finally they arrived at Capernaum and entered the home where they would lodge. To strip away their self-righteous veneer and reveal the pride that lay rotting beneath, Jesus asked a simple, soul-searching question. "What were you arguing about on the road?" A deafening silence filled the room. Heads tilted downward. Everyone avoided eye contact and secretly hoped Jesus would break the uncomfortable silence with a less threatening question. Not a chance. The silence dug its heels in and didn't budge an inch. Matthew cleared his throat. Philip stroked his shaggy beard. Andrew nervously crossed his arms—again. It was sure getting warm under those togas. Not a word was spoken.

In this uncomfortable moment, just when they thought Jesus might probe no further, he went straight for the heart. "If anyone wants to be first, he must be the very last, and servant of all." Then, to drive home the point, he used a vivid illustration. The master teacher grabbed a prop—a living one. A picture might be worth a thousand words, but a flesh-and-blood human being is a talking encyclopedia. The historian Luke records the moment.

> Jesus, knowing their thoughts, took a little child and had him stand beside him. Then he said to them, "Whoever welcomes this little child in my name welcomes me; and whoever welcomes me welcomes the one who sent me. For he who is least among you all—he is the greatest." (Luke 9:47-48)

A series of questions may have flashed through the disciples' minds. "What are my true motives? Do I want to serve others or manipulate them? Am I willing to humble myself like this child? Does the kingdom really work this way? If it does, can I ever hope to make it through the front gates?"

When our motives are exposed and we sit there vulnerable in the presence of the Holy One, what are our options? Denial? Excuses? Pretense? Hiding? Or would it be better to simply say, "That's me. I'm not proud of it, but it's part of who I am." Granted, it's an unnerving experience. To stand exposed before perfection leaves us ashamed and overwhelmed. But in the presence of Jesus, who knows our deepest thoughts and takes great pleasure in reshaping our darkest motives, we experience relief, freedom and joy.

And that's not a bad place to be—deeply known and fully loved.

❧ PERSONAL RESPONSE

What really motivates you—money, ego, love, pride, compassion, pain, fear? What drives you to act and think the way you do? If God could re-shape any of your motives, where might he begin?

❧ DIALOGUE WITH GOD

Jesus, I do not care for this introspective work. It's easier to groom the outside of my life than to clean up the inner world. I need you to teach me how to act, feel and think in life-giving ways. But I know that means you will poke around in places I wish to keep hidden. And you will find some junk—including that mirror I keep on the nightstand of my soul, just so I can remember who's most important in my life. Oh, I am so ashamed sometimes. Will you still love me if you really know me? I'm counting on it. That's my prayer.

❧ FURTHER BIBLE READING

Mark 8:31—9:37

THE TEACHER WHO CONFRONTS OUR UNBELIEF

Blessed are those who have not seen and yet have believed.

Trust. Belief. Rare commodities in Jesus' day, but even harder to find today. We are experiencing a credibility crisis that has touched every arena of life, from government and sports to business, entertainment, medicine, law, education and the church. University athletic programs are being investigated for NCAA violations, prominent corporations are scrutinized for fraud and accounting abuses, professional athletes are on trial for everything from sexual misconduct to murder, politicians are being chastised for breaking promises and mishandling tax dollars, church leaders are facing charges of sexual abuse, countless university students admit to cheating on exams, and police and firefighters are on the hot seat for fueling racial injustice. We need something to believe in, but where do we turn? Inevitably we begin to wonder, *Can anyone be trusted? Is there anyone left to believe in?*

When I was dating my lovely wife, Gail, I enjoyed discovering facts about her life—her past experiences, her youth in Panama, her work at IBM, her family and so on. But in order to really know her I had to take a step of faith. I had to trust her, to believe in her. I had to risk some self-disclosure and vulnerability. So finally I did it. I gave her my laundry. Really.

One night Gail wanted to get together for coffee, but I was just starting a load of wash that I had to get done. (I couldn't afford last month's strategy—buy another package of underwear and a new pair of jeans.) So she said, "Well, why don't you bring it over here and we can get some coffee and do it together." *Laundry? Together?*

I felt awkward but said yes because I hated doing laundry. I hated powdered soap, hot, stuffy laundromats, people who monopolized the place by separating their fabrics and colors until there were four items in each machine. Of course, I used the single man's guide to laundry separation—whites in one machine, everything else in the other. Repeat every thirty days.

So Gail and I did laundry. And I wondered whether she would still want to date me afterward. It's a vulnerable thing for a guy, letting a girl do his laundry—we can make some unsightly messes. But in a strange way it showed that there was trust, enough belief in each other and the progress of the relationship that this would be fun, not weird. And I realized that she was making a statement of trust and belief as well, getting involved in a personal area of my life that was neither glamorous nor exciting. After all, presoaking whites and spraying stain remover on grass stains is not like going to dinner and a show or taking a romantic walk through the arboretum. But in a silly way sharing the laundry marked a moment, a next step in the relationship. It made it safer for us to share more of our lives with each other.

Belief and trust are essential to intimacy and self-disclosure. The more we feel trusted and believed in, the more we are willing to reveal and the more we understand each other. I had to risk vulnerability and let Gail into my world. I had to believe she would honor me in the process—even when I did not have the facts to support that assumption. If we had waited to gather all the information, we'd never have gotten married.

When belief is absent and trust breaks down, skepticism creeps into a relationship, closely followed by a pervasive and debilitating cynicism. Doubt becomes the prevailing attitude, and we spend much of our emotional energy looking over our shoulder or behind our back. Once doubt reigns, it's hard to reweave the fabric of trust. It produces an endless cycle of uncertainty, hesitation, mistrust and suspicion. Everyone and everything is suspect. And that's dangerous.

Mark Buchanan describes the ultimate effect. "Here lies the basic flaw of all doubt: it can never really be satisfied. No evidence is ever fully, finally enough. Doubt wants always to consume, never to consummate. It clamors endlessly for an answer and so drowns out any answer that might be given it."

That's why Jesus talked so much about belief. Belief, not incessant doubting, opens the door to a knowledge deeper than facts can ever reveal. Though knowledge often produces a foundation for belief, like facts in a court case, it's also true that we must believe in order to discover true knowledge, particularly interpersonal knowledge.

We can study facts about Jesus all day—and there are plenty. But to know him more deeply we must risk believing some things: that we can actually have a relationship with God, that he is good, that he has our deepest interests at heart, that he can be trusted with our pain and shame, that he cares about our future, that he has incredible plans for us.

Belief is crucial to any growing relationship, and entering the company of Jesus is no different. With Jesus, belief is everything.

Because you have seen me, you have believed; blessed are those who have not seen and yet have believed. (John 20:29)

Everything is possible for him who believes. (Mark 9:23)

The work of God is this: to believe in the one he has sent. (John 6:29)

Whatever it is that fuels our unbelief, Jesus says it must be confronted. A persistent orientation of unbelief will harden the heart and put distance between us and him, ultimately hindering his work in us. Mark 6:5-6 says that when Jesus was in his hometown, "he could not do any miracles there. . . . And he was amazed at their lack of faith." Sad. The people of Nazareth never saw the mysterious and amazing work of God simply because they were unwilling to believe. He was willing to open his life and ministry to them, but like many of us, they chose to wallow in doubt.

Why do we often remain in disbelief? Why are we more like

Doubting Thomas than Daring Peter? Perhaps it's the thrill of the hunt; we like to pursue answers to complex issues and problems more than we like to receive the answers themselves. But more likely unbelief is a cover, a smoke screen, a captivating distraction. Sometimes it's easier to hide behind a mask of activity—intellectual activity, especially—rather than face the awkwardness of an uncomfortable or mysterious relationship. For habitual skeptics, no case is ever closed; no file is ever sealed.

But can we ever uncover enough data to overcome our unbelief? There are no stop signs in cyberspace, just an endless stream of on-ramps crowded with merging facts, data, survey results, proof-texts and downloads. The addictive quest for information and statistics can actually obscure the discovery of truth. Don't get me wrong; God is interested in facts—in truth, data, evidence—but not in facts alone. Data will point only to some forms of knowledge. For relational truth, if we aspire to know and be known, we must reach beyond the facts into the realm of belief.

Are you willing to believe Jesus? To trust him with your dirty laundry? To let him see the messy parts of your life? To put his teachings to the test—even the difficult sayings? Belief will open up a whole new world, filled with life and discoveries and learning you never thought possible. Jesus said, "I am the bread of life. He who comes to me will never go hungry, and he who believes in me will never be thirsty" (John 6:35).

PERSONAL RESPONSE

Why is it so hard for us to take relational risks, to believe in the unseen and unknown? Is there a pattern of relating that keeps you from believing that God will not let you down? How did you get to this point?

❧ DIALOGUE WITH GOD

Jesus, I want desperately to believe in you—to believe that you are the life-giver. I also want to trust you with my life—to open up and invite you into the mess that I sometimes am. But I confess it is a dice roll. I have believed others only to be disappointed. My gut says you will not do the same, but my head cries, "Don't fall for that again. You can't believe anyone!" From all I can see, you are worth the risk. So help me. I believe . . . help my unbelief.

❧ FURTHER BIBLE READING

John 5:31-47

THE TEACHER
WHO PRODS OUR TRANSFORMATION

Unless you change and become like little children,
you will never enter the kingdom of heaven.

When my daughter was four, our conversations went like this:

"Dad, what's a menno?"

"A what?"

"A menno. That's what you and Mommy say when you teach me the alphabet. Right in the middle you say, 'J, K, L, a menno, P.' So what's a menno?"

When my daughter turned seven, she asked me, "How do we believe in something we don't see?" She was skipping alongside me on a walk through our neighborhood.

"What made you ask that?" I said.

"Well, if there really is a God, why can't we see him?"

Wow! My daughter was growing up fast. Now she had hard questions.

The next few minutes were amazing. While she skipped along the asphalt, I was walking on air, lost in the joy of a natural and effortless conversation. As I grasped her trusting hand we walked and talked, two pilgrims on the road to truth. We arrived home and sat on the bench under our magnolia tree, looking at the shimmering pond that lay across the road. We talked about how God reveals himself in true, easy-to-see ways in his people, his words and in his creation. It was a moment I will always treasure.

Become like a child. A child's questions are rooted in an honest, probing sincerity that dissipates much too rapidly as adulthood approaches. No pretense or hidden agenda, no posturing for position and power, not a hint of pharisaic manipulation designed to trap or befuddle. Just plain, simple and direct. Like the faith Jesus said is required to fully participate in the freedom-filled life of the kingdom.

> Unless you change and become like little children, you will never enter the kingdom of heaven. (Matthew 18:3)

Unless you change? Yes.

Matthew, the Gospel writer and an inner-circle friend of Jesus, uses a word that means "to turn around" or "to head in the opposite direction." It has the same root as our word *catastrophe*, which literally means "a turning down, an upheaval." Becoming childlike does not mean pursuing foolish ambition or shirking adult responsibility. Rather, it is a turning away from old patterns. It requires that we reject all that is superficial and pretentious, stripping away the corrosion from the surface of the soul to reveal the authentic inner self.

> I'm telling you, once and for all, that unless you return to

square one and start over like children, you're not even going to get a look at the kingdom, let alone get in. (Matthew 18:3 *The Message*)

In other words, we need a catastrophic change of heart!

Few experiences rival the unabashed embrace of a child's greeting after a long trip or a frazzling day of work. "Mommy's home!" or "Daddy's back!" fills the air while thirty-two inches of rampaging joy comes bounding across the room at a hundred miles per hour. With unfettered faith this volcano of energy leaps fearlessly into your outstretched arms, shrink-wrapping herself against your body. In that moment—those few seconds you wish would last an eternity—you have a glimpse of what Jesus means. Your child was occupied and distracted by play or schoolwork when you entered the home. But soon she stops and turns at the sound of your voice, rushing into your safe, strong embrace, fully convinced of your incessant love.

Jesus longs for this from every child of his—a turn at the sound of his voice and the prompting of his truth. A turn that produces change. A turn that takes us back to our childlike roots. And, if necessary, a return to a private burial ground where we must exhume our decaying faith, hope and love from the cold ground. As Brennan Manning reminds us, we must return to a belief system that links truth with experience.

In contemporary Christianity there is an essential difference between belief and faith. Our religious beliefs are the visible expression of our faith, our personal commitment to the person of Jesus. However, if the Christian beliefs inherited from our family and passed on to us by our church tradition are not grounded in a shattering, life-changing experience of Jesus as the Christ, then the chasm between our creedal statements and our own faith-experience widens and our witness is worthless. The gospel will persuade no one unless it has so convicted us that we are transformed by it.

Transformation. That's the buzzword of the age. Question: How many infomercials promise total transformation? Answer: All of them. It's the ultimate hook, the supreme come-on, the tantalizing bait dangled before every late-night tube watcher. "It will change your life. Just six minutes a day, three days a week. That's all. Try it for thirty days and if you're not satisfied, we'll refund your money." What's not to like about that deal? Change is easy and virtually guaranteed!

Who really wants to change their life? I'll tell you who—no one. Not really. Oh, we all think we want to change, or we would like the benefits of change, but few of us are committed to the process. I am the first to admit how difficult this is. Change is hard. So we become easy prey for the "change without pain" strategies pitched our way. (Which is why we all have some piece of exercise equipment gathering dust in the dark recesses of the garage or attic, ripening up for the next garage sale.)

We need transformation, but we cannot change ourselves by ourselves. Therein lies the paradox. We need help. Jesus promises to transform us from the inside out, but here's the deal—we have to become like kids while he does the work of God. His part is easy, because he's God. Our part is difficult because it requires humility and vulnerability, something few of us majored in at college. But it can be done if we cultivate a willing and obedient heart that makes the effort to be receptive to the work of God. It's a divine and mysterious partnership. "Continue to work out your salvation with fear and trembling," wrote Paul to a young church, "for it is God who works in you to will and to act according to his good purpose" (Philippians 2:12-13).

It requires effort for maturing adults to pursue spiritual growth while taking on the inquisitive posture of a child. In order to change in this way, we listen carefully to others on the faith journey toward Christ, we read the Bible with enthusiasm and worship God with a sense of wonder and awe, we ask his Spirit to change us, we pay attention to his promptings and we serve others humbly. In effect, we joyfully position ourselves in the places and activities where God is at work, and we strive to remain there against every distraction that would woo us away.

I am reminded of a commercial from the 1980s. It was an advertisement promoting travel to Jamaica, and it portrayed the fun, excitement, laughter and freedom available to anyone longing for a tropical getaway. The ad ended with these words, spoken with a Jamaican accent: "Come to Jamaica—and become a child again."

Jesus' words are similar, but his promise is much more profound. Instead of promoting a temporary lifestyle, Jesus offers an amazing way of life. In place of a brief stay at a tropical playland, he invites us to spend forever in a heavenly paradise. Instead of simply treating us like kings, he offers the keys to the kingdom. It's all ours, free of charge, including airfare. There's only one condition: "Let the little children come to me, and do not hinder them, for the kingdom of God belongs to such as these. I tell you the truth, anyone who will not receive the kingdom of God like a little child will never enter it" (Luke 18:16-17).

C'mon, let's go. Come to Jesus—and become a child again.

PERSONAL RESPONSE

What is standing in the way of change for you? Is it an attitude, a habit or the consequences of a poor decision? Do you believe that God can change you, and are you willing to work with him?

🦌 DIALOGUE WITH GOD

Dear God, it is hard for me to put childish ways behind me and yet become childlike. Part of me wants to grow up—and part of me wants to be a kid forever, without weighty responsibilities and momentous decisions at every turn. I know that's nonsense. Perhaps this is a new way— a childlike posture combined with an adult work ethic. Humility and openness coupled with a persevering spirit. A recognition that you must first work in me, and a determination to change the patterns and habits that hinder that work. This is going to be hard. But it's worth it. So change me, I pray.

🦌 FURTHER BIBLE READING

Romans 12

Jesus

OUR SACRED FRIEND

In the eyes of the first-century spiritual elite, Jesus was a conundrum. His life was a thousand-piece puzzle with no photo on the box, and they failed miserably every time they tried to put it together. His provocative and disarming teaching confounded them, and his choice of friends unnerved them—Jesus, the "friend of sinners."

Jesus seemed to take great pleasure in befriending people on the Pharisees' Ten Most Unwanted list. These pious and perfectionist patriarchs burst into fits of rage every time Jesus connected with someone on their list. Unscrupulous tax collectors, untouchable lepers, unclean prostitutes, unlearned fishermen, undesirable Samaritans and uncouth Roman soldiers regularly found their faces on posters throughout Jerusalem marked "Unwanted: Dead or Alive." But remarkably—and incredibly—these same faces consistently found themselves sitting alongside Jesus at the table of community. But that shouldn't be surprising, unless you're a Pharisee. As Brennan Man-

ning remarks, Jesus never really was a social climber; he often enter-
tained "sinner-guests" at his table.

Like the Pharisees, Jesus also had a list, a kind of "Who's Not Who
in the Ancient World." Jesus had friends in low places. Broken people, sinful people, unattractive and despised people. A true friend of
sinners was this Jesus—and he still is. He's a friend to people who
love their kids but cut corners on their taxes. People who work over-
time at the office but can't find an hour to serve the poor. People who
abhor the tragedy of homelessness but flood their minds with the
sewage from TV sets and theaters.

If we're honest, we have to admit that this is who we are—double-
minded, conflicted, lonely and in desperate need of a friend, especially
a loving and forgiving one. We need a grace-giving companion who will
receive us in spite of ourselves. Or as Henry Ward Beecher has said,
"Every man should have a fair-sized cemetery in which to bury the
faults of his friends." In the moment Jesus takes us as his companions,
he dons the overalls of a gravedigger, covering our shattered, sinful past
with the soil of divine mercy. A true friend . . . that's what we need.

Jesus the Christ is our sacred friend. He is someone who has the
spiritual fortitude to confront our wretchedness without shrinking
back in disgust. Someone who will tolerate our flailing fits of rage
when we cannot have our way. Someone who is willing to cast aside
the privileges of divine Sonship in order to embrace our fallen humanity with joy and laughter. A friend who, despite being greater,
lets us in on the secrets of heaven.

> I'm no longer calling you servants because servants don't un-
> derstand what their master is thinking and planning. No, I've
> named you friends because I've let you in on everything I've
> heard from the Father. (John 15:15 *The Message*)

In this sacred bond of friendship, the majestic Jesus becomes one of us. He loses neither honor nor status but humbly hides it from full view. He is now "my friend, the king." I must confess to a whimsical joy that permeates my soul as I reflect on that truth. This sacred, divine, kingly God-man is also my friend, a partner and guide in this troublesome life. He chooses this friendship without condescension or compulsion, eagerly seeking the companionship of wayward sinners like me. He wants to share his life with me, and desires mine in return. You will never find a more remarkable and intimate friendship.

Let me elaborate on this idea of friendship with God focused on the person of Jesus. For some of us it sounds almost heretical. God is distant, powerful, holy and wholly other. It's hard to view him apart from his majesty. Perhaps for others the idea isn't heretical—just impossible. Not because of who God is but because of what we have become. Familiar messages play inside our heads, recurring echoes of past voices that shout, *Why would God have any interest in someone like you? Why would Jesus want to spend even five minutes with you after what you've done?* Don't give in to these voices, and don't yield to contrived heresy. Friendship with you and me is God's idea, not ours. He makes the first move, he takes the first steps—and he keeps pressing toward us.

When we left Dallas in 1992 for Chicago and my new position at Willow Creek, it had taken eleven months to sell our home. This shattered many of our illusions. (Remember that false belief I mentioned earlier, "If God wants us to move, he will help us sell our home quickly"?) We had sold our previous home in ten minutes to the first person who looked at it. So we expected similar treatment from God this time. After all, we were just as convinced we were in the center of his will. But a devastating oil and gas crisis weakened the regional economy and crippled the real estate market in Dallas.

So it was seven months before we received an offer. Naturally, we were elated.

One month later, just days before closing the sale, I received a phone call from our agent. I was packing one of the last boxes for the moving van as she explained that the buyers had failed to secure adequate financing. The deal was off. We had to unpack, put the pictures back on the walls, and start showing the home to buyers again. It had been eight months now, and we were nowhere. My wife and I sat on the bed bewildered and devastated, asking ourselves and God questions that had no answers. We desperately needed a friend, a sacred friend. Someone who understood our pain and yet had the power to restore our wounded souls. Our Dallas friends and family had been supportive and wonderful during the ordeal. But we needed friendship with God that transcended all human capacity. That deep, satisfying friendship was centered in Christ.

He was with me two months later when I departed for Chicago, with my family in the rearview mirror and still no contract on our Dallas home. He was whispering, "Trust me. I'm doing a work in you. And I will take care of you and your family." Two weeks later, in month eleven, we were able to sell the home and move.

In those last few months of intense waiting, I discovered a deeper reality in my friendship with Christ, one wrought by frustration and forged in pain. To this day I revel in this relationship, amazed at how intimate and inspiring it can be. I discovered I can really depend on him—not just for selling a house, but for grace, courage and strength. I deepened the relationship I discovered with him when I was twenty-three. This new encounter, this turning point, was another chance to grow and mature in the company of Jesus.

A Friend Who Shares Our Suffering

Because he himself suffered when he was tempted,
he is able to help those who are being tempted.

The twenty-four hours before our first child arrived was no picnic, especially since the objective was "natural childbirth." It was excruciatingly painful, exhausting and demanding, requiring every ounce of emotional, physical and spiritual strength. At times it was utterly chaotic—doctors and nurses hovering about, checking vital signs, bringing water, making decisions. Nausea, sweating, chills and moments of sheer panic were constant companions. It was horrible.

But enough about my experience—let's talk about what happened to my wife.

Gail desired natural childbirth (versus "unnatural," in which the baby is delivered by UPS), so we "invested" sixty dollars in six weeks of natural childbirth classes. A petite young instructor named Kelly taught us that this experience would be wonderful, honor God's design and be relatively pain-free if Gail breathed the right way. (Kelly had already birthed five children this way in as many years, never gaining any weight, going back to work in two days, jogging after a week and loving every minute of it—"even the moment my water broke!") Fathers-to-be were instructed to hold up an index finger at the onset of a contraction to get our wife's attention and help her regain focus. Then we were to count rhythmically using our fingers, helping her pace her breathing. One, two, three . . . phew, phew, phew. It was all so simple. Gail and I performed well and got an A in the class.

At the hospital I stood alongside my wife in the birthing room. Despite what you might see on TLC's *A Baby Story*, this is not every guy's dream. Oh, seeing the baby arrive is a wonderful thing. Sign me up. But those hours before the arrival are another matter. The first major contraction hit and Gail began to writhe and moan. This was the moment of truth, the moment we had been trained for; six weeks of practice were about to pay off. Gail's breathing became erratic, so I held up my finger—and she grabbed it. This was not what we were taught in class. I have the video to prove it. Then she bent my finger. Ever notice how fingers are designed to bend one way and not others?

Gail was failing to honor the God-given anatomical design of my index finger. When my yelling matched hers in both pitch and volume, she relented and I gained my composure. I tried to offer some comforting words. Perhaps a few insights, a short poem or a Bible verse would ease her suffering.

"Shhh!" was her response. This was also not taught in class. "Please, just stand here and hold my hand." As I stood there, I saw sixty dollars fly out the window along with Kelly's smiling face. After a few moments, when the contraction had faded, I decided to try speaking again. This idea left the room as quickly as my sixty bucks. Gail wanted my presence in her suffering, not my words or suggestions. She wanted a pain partner. I needed to realize that quickly— and she helped me along. That's why she's the better half.

Deep, enduring relationships are not built on the shifting sands of convenience or camaraderie—they are forged through pain, sacrifice and commitment. Something that separates Christianity from all other religious systems is that its founder chose to befriend his followers by suffering with them and dying for them. The road to the cross in Jerusalem is called the *Via Dolorosa*—the Way of Suffering. True friends are pain partners. But Jesus was even more. When he died in our place he moved beyond partner to Savior.

But we see Jesus, who was made a little lower than the angels,
now crowned with glory and honor because he suffered death,
so that by the grace of God he might taste death for everyone.
(Hebrews 2:9)

As you read this, somewhere on this planet people are suffering
simply because they follow Jesus. On November 21, 2002, American
missionary Bonnie Witherall, thirty-one, was gunned down in Lebanon at the prenatal clinic where she worked. A graduate of Moody
Bible Institute in Chicago, she and her husband had been serving in
Lebanon two years. Gary Witherall forgives his wife's killer. "Christ's
blood was poured out for us. Bonnie's blood was poured out for the
women of Sidon, all over that clinic floor."

Experts estimate that 250 million Christians worldwide suffer under oppressive regimes. In Burma, ranked by the U.S. State Depart-
ment as one of the six worst violators of religious freedom, live four
million persecuted Christians. Burma has the dubious distinction of
experiencing the world's longest-running civil war, which has resulted in atrocities toward Christians since World War II. A typical
story is that of a Burmese town where the church was torched, crops
burned, homes set ablaze and a clinic demolished. Villagers had to
escape when they spotted the military or be subjected to rape, murder or forced labor. Says the pastor of this church, "We have to leave
village after village, house after house. But it increases our faith. We
are Christians; we know God will help us. But please remember us in
your prayers. Please do not forget."

Let us absorb that plea. Let us not forget to suffer with our Burmese brothers and sisters . . . to mourn with those who mourn . . . to
partner with them in their pain.

There are many things we like to share with close friends—ballgame tickets, laughter, food, vacations, carpool duties, recipes, power tools, favorite movies. Suffering usually doesn't make the list. But sharing in suffering was a trademark of the early Jesus community. It was not sought after in a morbid or macabre way, like many whose self-inflicted suffering is a means to appease their gods. But it was endured and shared as a means of union with Christ, a pathway to intimacy with the suffering Jesus. Most likely his words echoed in their hearts when the heavy hand of oppression and tyranny struck with all its might.

> Blessed are you when people insult you, persecute you and falsely say all kinds of evil against you because of me. Rejoice and be glad, because great is your reward in heaven, for in the same way they persecuted the prophets who were before you. (Matthew 5:11-12)

Writing from prison, the apostle Paul longed "to know Christ and the power of his resurrection and the fellowship of sharing in his sufferings" (Philippians 3:10). I must confess, I like the "power of his resurrection" part. Can we just stick with that and forget the suffering? But I know I cannot have one without the other. When I share the life and friendship of Jesus, I share all of him. And when I become part of his body—the church—I share in the fullness of that body.

Our shared suffering with Jesus creates an eternal bond. Like war veterans gathered at a reunion to recount their triumphs and tragedies, there exists a deep-seated and profound sense of oneness. Outsiders can neither fully appreciate it nor share in it completely. But that's what I love about Jesus. He's no outsider to our experience of suffering. He lived an embattled life and is well acquainted with grief; he's a man of sorrows. He's not a guest at the reunion—he's the most decorated veteran.

By contrast, imagine a leader who comes to a weak and disenfranchised group of sufferers and asks, "How's everyone doing today?" After hearing the despairing replies, the leader responds, "Wow, that's really tough. I wish life were better for you. As for me, I just got back from three weeks in Hawaii, all expenses paid, and as you can see I have a great tan. My kids are doing very well—all A's in school and college scholarship offers lining up at the door. Just yesterday I collected a ten-thousand-dollar bonus and was given a new corner office at work. And because I've been working out at the fitness center the last few months, I feel as strong and healthy as I was when I was nineteen! Life is awesome. But wow, I sure do empathize with all of you. I know it must be hard."

Let's take a guess. Do you think these people, after hearing that, are drawn closer to this leader? Do they feel a deep sense of community with him or her? Would they find the leader approachable and sympathetic? I think you can figure it out.

Joni Eareckson Tada was paralyzed in a diving accident she sustained just after high school graduation. Her steadfast perseverance and unwavering endurance in the face of despair and suffering have made her an inspiration to millions worldwide. Her artwork (painstakingly painted by mouth), her public speaking, TV interviews, her autobiographical book *Joni* and a movie of her life all launched her into the public limelight, where she has been a tireless and aggressive spokesperson for the rights and plight of the disabled community. A *Christianity Today* interview with Joni reveals her frame of mind.

> I was heading down a path to self-destruction. I was checking out a birth-control clinic to get some pills, because I knew I'd be sleeping with my boyfriend in college. Somewhere in that mess of emotions and regrets and falterings and failings, while

making a sham of my Christian faith, somewhere in the desperation I said, "God, rescue me." And he did. I believe my accident was a direct answer. Some people might want to say indirect, but I lean toward that old adage that God draws straight lines with crooked sticks.

Joni asserts that God permits suffering in our lives to drive us toward him, and that broken, disabled, needy people are a gift to the church. "I love the bride of Christ, but there are an awful lot of Emily Post picture-perfect churches out there," she says. "Ministry is messy. God plops people with disabilities in the midst of a congregation—a hand grenade that blows apart the picture-perfectness of these churches. So what will the church do? Will it embrace these people?"

Sufferers connect with Joni because her weary feet have traveled the pathway of pain. No sappy slogans or trite witticisms come from her lips. Her words, like her faith, are raw and gritty yet laced with grace toward a broken world.

You are a sufferer. I am a sufferer. And the church—if it is authentic—must confess it is filled with struggling sufferers, bearing our collective disabilities together under a banner carried by the Man of Sorrows. The One who suffered physically, emotionally and spiritually with us and for us is there to accompany us. After all, everyone needs a pain partner.

PERSONAL RESPONSE

Pain is lessened when it is shared. Could it be that your present suffering is a pathway to intimacy with God? Perhaps you walk a personal Via Dolorosa, and you need a partner to carry your cross with you on "the way of suffering." Even Jesus needed that. Are you willing to ask?

❧ DIALOGUE WITH GOD

God, I withdraw at the thought of suffering. I shrink back at the mention of pain, let alone the experience. How can a loving and caring Father allow his kids to suffer? It is so unconventional, so countercultural. I do not know what to make of it. But this I can say. You have shown yourself to be reliable in other areas. In this very difficult area, where comprehension takes a back seat to bewilderment, I am going to risk trusting—trusting that if I give you my pain, you will help carry it. So here I go.

❧ FURTHER BIBLE READING

Mark 15:1-41

A FRIEND WHO DESIRES OUR FELLOWSHIP

. . . that he might be with them.

At a leadership gathering some years ago our leadership team at Willow Creek coined the phrase "the 'be with' factor," handing out T-shirts with those words on the logo. It was group-speak for fellowship, for community. In ancient Greek it's *koinonia;* in South Africa my friends call it *ubuntu.* It connotes a shared life of intimacy, friendship and mutual concern. It involves more than simply hanging out, but it can't be achieved unless some hanging out happens. It begins when someone drops by or calls or says, "Let's get coffee." And it extends to every area of life in which "we" becomes more common than "me." Unfortunately, this kind of fellowship is a rare phenomenon in the States.

"You Americans move around a lot," observed my Swiss friend.

"Yes, we do," I agreed.

"It must be hard to maintain friendships," he continued.

"No, not really," I quipped. "People who move a lot don't invest in friendships, so there's nothing to maintain."

Here's the reality. Our pursuit of the American dream produces relational nightmares for the 20 percent of citizens who move in any given year. For some the pursuit is almost pathological, a rabid hunt for success at the expense of kids, friends and family ties. For others it's the unavoidable consequence of job losses in a shifting economy.

Military families experience the syndrome in disproportionate doses. A U.S. Army chaplain recently told me of his own childhood in a military family, during which he attended fifteen schools in twelve years. He observes today how families desperately desire fellowship when they arrive on the base. "They know if deep friendships don't form quickly, they won't have time to make any at all—a pattern they fear will follow them indefinitely."

So, in this community-starved culture where significant friendships are harder to find than cheap gas at the pump, being invited into fellowship with another person meets a deep craving. Sadly, few of us ever receive an invitation that reads, "The pleasure of your company is requested." Unless, of course, it's to Cousin Rita's wedding, whom you haven't seen since fourth grade but who is secretly hoping you'll drop a fifty-dollar gift in the mail.

"The pleasure of your company." It's a wonderful phrase.

The summer I graduated from college two roommates and I traveled across the country to "see America" before beginning jobs or heading off to graduate school. We mapped our itinerary with two priorities in mind: keen points of interest (Niagara Falls, Yellowstone Park, the Badlands and so on), and free places to eat and sleep. We camped out in national parks or stayed at the homes of college buddies or relatives (or relatives of college buddies, or distant relatives of people who once knew someone who might have been a friend of a college buddy).

Outside Chicago, where we had visited the Sears Tower, we stayed with our college friend Peter, his gracious mother and his younger sister. Upon arrival we were met with the exuberant hugs and loud greetings of a classic Italian American family. As we sat down to dinner, we faced at least ten pounds of Italian sausage and mountains of bread. Three of us, including Peter, had been involved in football and track at the university, so it looked like she'd prepared a training meal for ravenous athletes. I was amazed at the volume of food for just the six of us. Peter's family exchanged Italian gestures and expressions throughout dinner, making us feel like we'd stepped into the Old Country outside Rome or Venice.

After we finished Peter invited us to the family room, where we reclined in bloated bliss. Ahhh. What a feast! After about fifteen minutes Peter shouted, "Ready Mama?" Yes . . . dessert—just as I'd hoped. I was glad I'd left some room.

Upon re-entering the dining room I saw a large salad beside a huge bowl of pasta and a tray of about two hundred meatballs soaked in marinara sauce. "Wow, momma, this looks great!" Peter said. "Are you guys ready for the second course?"

Second course? I was still processing sausage number five from course number one! How many courses would there be? This one alone equaled the amount of food we'd consumed at my family reunion for thirty-five people last year.

Over the next four hours we consumed four courses, followed by dessert—actually, three desserts—all separated by ten-minute interludes for conversation and digestion. (I took advantage of those times to recover like a boxer sitting in the corner between rounds, trying to catch my breath and prepare for the next bout of competition.)

I asked Peter why his mother had made so much food for us. We were honored, but she had overdone it. "Oh, she does this every Sunday," he said—like it was no big deal. "She cooks all this food, and then we eat it all week long. But this allows us to sample it and have time to be together."

Time together. The "be with" factor, with food as the excuse. This family understood fellowship.

As I reflect back, I realize that fellowship was precisely what the afternoon was designed for—time to be together, to talk and enjoy one another. Peter and his family had eaten reasonable portions, pacing themselves so they could enjoy the pleasure of our company. We had missed the point. This was not an eating contest or a chance for Peter's mother to impress us with her culinary abilities or presentation skills. The food and décor were simple yet inviting. The atmosphere was warm, the conversation personal. We had been invited to the table of community, and we had almost missed it.

Jesus desires our fellowship. Without pretense he invites us to join him. Look at what he said to his closest followers.

I have eagerly desired to eat this Passover with you before I suffer. (Luke 22:15)

He appointed twelve—designating them apostles—that they might be with him. (Mark 3:14)

If anyone loves me, he will obey my teaching. My Father will love him, and we will come to him and make our home with him. (John 14:23)

This invitation is extended today, every day, to ordinary fellowship-starved people like us. Come—there is an open chair at the table, and the place card has your name on it.

✌ PERSONAL RESPONSE

We long for deep connection with others yet fear it at the same time. Why? And the same is true of God. We long for his fellowship but sometimes wonder if he's interested in cavorting with folks like us. After reading this, has your view of God and his desire to be with you changed?

✌ DIALOGUE WITH GOD

God, I would love to hang out with you, but it feels so awkward. After all, you are God—King, Lord, Master. And yet you are Friend, Servant and Helper as well. It scares me. You understand everything about me while I feel like a first-grader in a graduate class. The playing field is not level. I can't believe you actually enjoy time with me. What do I have to offer? I don't bring much to the table besides my bumps and bruises, my insecurities and doubts, my excuses and shortcomings. That's enough, you say? Just me? I love the sound of it, but I confess it's hard to believe. Well, OK . . . here I am. I'm grateful you invited me to your table. Please excuse my manners. This is still new for me. Help me honor your character but still embrace your offer for intimacy. Please help me lift my head and look you in the eye, and remember that you see me for what I can become instead of what I am today. Thanks for loving me.

✌ FURTHER BIBLE READING

Psalm 23

A FRIEND WHO GUARDS OUR TRUST

Do not let your hearts be troubled. Trust in God; trust also in me.

"I will be sure—always!" Not a particularly dynamic statement at first glance. It doesn't make the chest swell with national pride like "For honor, country and king!" It doesn't have an abrasive edge like "Lead, follow or get out the way!" And it doesn't awaken a sense of camaraderie like "One for all—and all for one!" evokes in people's hearts (especially Musketeer lovers).

The slogan belongs to a special unit within the Texas Air National Guard, a group of workers known as Riggers. What makes "I will be sure—always!" a particularly profound slogan for this unit?

Riggers pack parachutes. They meticulously fold and pack the canopy of every M1A1 military parachute—the kind a U.S. Army Airborne jumper uses when leaping from a transport plane at five thousand feet. It takes twenty minutes to make the thirty precise folds required to pack the chute properly. The Riggers' motto elaborates on their philosophy: "I will never let the idea that a piece of work is 'good enough' cause me to become a murderer through a careless mistake or oversight. I know there can be no compromise with perfection."

Imagine standing at the open bay of a C-41 transport plane in full battle gear with eighty pounds of equipment strapped to your body, everything you need to survive for ten days in hazardous or hostile conditions. You glance below. One more step and you will be jerked around by 140-mile-per-hour winds. Dropping like a 250-pound rock you will descend at a rate of 220 feet per second, a slave to the force of gravity, which promises to plant your body firmly in earth's soil at a speed of 165 miles an hour. Only one thing can keep you from becoming some farmer's fertilizer—that big, white, thirty-foot canopy: your parachute.

But here's the catch. You didn't fold or pack that canopy. You didn't check the ripcord or inspect the rigging, didn't search for rips, repair any defects or look for signs of premature shredding. Besides that, you've never even met the person who packed it. You just picked it up and strapped it on. Right now as you leap into the air, the person who packed your chute is probably washing down bacon and eggs with a hot cup of coffee, or kissing his wife goodbye as he ushers the kids out the front door for soccer practice, or cheering for his favorite ball team.

So as you take a deep breath and step into the airy abyss between you and your favorite planet, you're banking on one thing. When you pull that cord, a parachute comes out. Not an umbrella or a blanket or a paper sack with some kid's sandwich in it.

Airborne jumpers exercise great faith—they believe in a proven training system and implicitly trust a group of perfection-obsessed, parachute-packing Riggers. Riggers who are in training have to personally jump with every chute they pack (some extra motivation to "get it right"). Riggers know what it means to put their own lives on the line, and to put hands and feet on that not-so-trivial slogan: "I will be sure—always!"

What happens if you and I put our lives in the hands of Jesus of Nazareth? Can he be trusted? Oh, I don't think he'll lie or cheat or steal from us. And I doubt he'll intentionally deceive us or make us the brunt of an embarrassing practical joke. But are we sure he's placed a trustworthy parachute in the satchel he's just handed us, the one marked, "Trust me!"?

Shards of shattered trust are strewn across the terrain of our contemporary culture. Deception reigns, at least for a season, until it is uncovered. At this point we self-righteously feign shock and shake our heads in mock disbelief. Inwardly we shudder, knowing it could easily have been us revealed as the deceiver. Deceptive, trust-busting behavior is on the rise.

"Has America become a nation of cheaters?" asks a *U.S. News & World Report* article, citing how broadly the disease of deception has spread. Here are a few examples from the article.

- Seventy-four percent of high school students admit to serious cheating on tests, double the number admitting such behavior in 1969.

- The chairman of Sotheby's, the elite auction house, is sentenced to one year in jail for a price-fixing scheme involving artwork that cost customers one hundred million dollars.

- A Pulitzer Prize winner remains banned from teaching at Mount Holyoke College for fabricating a story that he was a Vietnam veteran.

- A Notre Dame coach is fired after five days because of lies found on his resumé.

- Americans cheat the tax code every year—about 1600 dollars per person—mounting to a whopping 195 billion dollars in lost revenue.

So the writers ask, "What's going on here? Does anyone play by the rules?"

Can we trust anyone—including God?

I have watched thousands of people jump into the faith void, guided only by the assurance of what God has already done and the likelihood that he will be the same God in the future. Each person pulled the ripcord on the satchel Jesus strapped to their backs, and each one has landed safely. No disastrous freefalls, tangled chutes or crash landings. Sometimes the headwinds are strong. And sometimes the enemy is shooting from below. But as they step into the danger zone they hear the echo of Jesus' voice saying, "I will never leave you nor forsake you." You can count on that. He will be sure—always.

✤ PERSONAL RESPONSE

Has anyone violated your trust? Then you know the pain and anger that come with betrayal. Jesus, whose betrayal was acted out on a grand scale before a sold-out crowd, is fully aware of your feelings and fears. You have a choice—to risk trusting again, or to shrink back into the dark corner of self-pity and resentment. What would it take for you to take a trust leap with Jesus?

✤ DIALOGUE WITH GOD

First, God, I have a confession. I know I have been betrayed, but I have also played the role of Judas, selling someone's trust for a lot less than thirty pieces of silver. I have treated trust like loose change in a pocketful of holes. It has hurt me and disappointed others. Maybe that's why I'm so fearful. Will you handle my trust like I have stewarded the confidence of others? Or will you be different? Will you guard and protect my trust like a collector of fine jewels, or cast it like pearls before swine? No, I doubt you'll ever do that. So here I go. I trust you now—with my fears and my fate. I'm pulling the cord—and praying. Not because I doubt you, but because I need you. After all, what options do I have?

✤ FURTHER BIBLE READING

John 14:1-14

A FRIEND WHO RECOGNIZES OUR WEAKNESS

A time is coming, and has come, when you will be scattered,
each to his own home. You will leave me all alone.

We have a Sheltie at home that looks like Lassie minus a few growth hormones. We have a love-hate relationship. She loves me; I hate her. Well, not exactly. It's just that she bugs the socks off me sometimes.

Historically used as herding dogs, shelties have been bred to incessantly circle a flock until all the sheep are bunched together. This is their mission in life, and they are terribly insecure if they cannot accomplish it. In the absence of sheep, like at our house, shelties will settle for children playing in the yard or adults walking through the kitchen.

That's what bugs me—being stalked by a two-foot-high animal that mistakes me for a sheep. One day, amidst particularly persistent stalking and intense panting (a miserable combo), I yelled "Go!" and our dog fled under the table, only to return two minutes later, stalking and panting. I couldn't stand it any longer. So I locked her in a small, dark closet with no food or water for two days. Well, not really. But it did cross my mind. I never said I was perfect.

Actually, I placed her in our three-by-eight-foot laundry room until she calmed down. As I closed the door she looked up at me with her pouty eyes, ears flattened back against her head. There she sat, left behind, discarded like a dirty penny, ashamed and forlorn. Don't worry, she had food and water and eventually I let her out. She's really not so bad—except for the stalking.

Ever feel locked up and second-rate? Or discarded like an old shoe along the side of the road? Maybe your behavior was the cause, or your skin color, or your ethnic background or socioeconomic status. Perhaps your friends have a love-hate relationship with you. They love you when you perform on cue, and hate you when you've served your purpose for the moment. Just when you think you fit in and have been accepted, you get the cold shoulder and no one makes eye contact with you at the party.

Rejection. Criticism. Betrayal. These are the instruments of relational torture. In the hands of the skillfully wicked or blithely ignorant they can inflict mortal wounds to the soul, leaving behind a dull aching pain covered by layers of scar tissue. Rather than placing ourselves in the hands of the Great Physician and in the company of his wounded friends, we opt for self-diagnosis and treatment. Unskilled and seeking immediate relief, we try to medicate the pain and camouflage the scars. In so doing we avoid not only the emergency room, but the rehabilitation center as well. We are the victims of a hit-and-run, but we leave the scene of the accident before the ambulance arrives. After all, we do not want our pictures in the paper, our bloodied faces on the six o'clock news. Someone we know might see us. We exchange healing community in the company of Jesus for shrouded secrecy.

Larry Crabb says, "We protect our wounds with all the fierceness of a lioness watching over her cubs. And because it is nearly impossible to see who we are as separate from these wounds, we think we are protecting our selves when in fact we are preserving our wounds."

We are masters of the art of deception, sophisticated at denying weakness and hiding injury. Even in Third World countries where physical problems are more obvious, it's customary to hide weakness out of fear of rejection. In South Africa HIV-positive people say they have tuberculosis, because TB is an "acceptable" illness free from the stigma of AIDS.

We are *sophisticated*, a word from a Greek root that means "to play the sophist," which refers to a practice in which Greek teachers articulated clever (and sometimes false) arguments in order to make a point. Another way of saying it is "refined to the point of artificiality." Are we too refined, too cultured to admit what many, especially God, already know? Isn't it better to admit, as many spiritual guides through the ages have affirmed, that we are broken, but we are loved?

You need never hide your pain and scars from the man with the nail-pierced hands. Do not hide your weakness from Jesus, the friend of the weak.

> He was despised and rejected by men,
>> a man of sorrows, and familiar with suffering. . . .
> He took up our infirmities
>> and carried our sorrows. (Isaiah 53:3-4)

Brokenness—weakness—was a way of life for Jesus, and it produced hope and strength. That's a virtual heresy in this material world where health and wealth prophets (or is that "profits"?) have prematurely exchanged rugged crosses for royal crowns. Paul said, "I preach Christ and him crucified," not "I preach man and him rewarded." The symbol of weakness that all can embrace has been traded for the specter of wealth in which only a few can share.

Yes, Jesus loves me. And yes, he recognizes me—under all the makeup. He knows that I am weak, just like the Twelve who closely followed his every move and hung on every sacred word. He knows that under the right pressure and in the right circumstance, I will deny his name, betray his trust, turn and run. Just like they did. Because I am weak, just like they were.

But when we return to the company of Jesus, as they ultimately did, having traded our selfish sophistication for a contrite humility, we discover we are broken—and we are loved. That our wounds, like those of Jesus, are beautiful reminders of the loving grace of God.

> But he said to me, "My grace is sufficient for you, for my power is made perfect in weakness." Therefore I will boast all the more gladly about my weaknesses, so that Christ's power

may rest on me. That is why, for Christ's sake, I delight in weaknesses, in insults, in hardships, in persecutions, in difficulties. For when I am weak, then I am strong. (2 Corinthians 12:9-10)

As much as I love those words, I shrink back from putting my weaknesses out there for the world to see. Our men's small group is in the midst of studying 2 Corinthians, a book replete with references to weakness and brokenness. Just last week we wrestled with the truth that God is often at his best when we are our weakest. It is absolutely countercultural, yet we are called to live there. Beyond that, we are called to thrive there!

But what does living in weakness look like? How does an executive at a major corporation practice this? What does an attorney do with this truth as he argues cases and deposes witnesses? And what does a pastor do who must lead people and inspire them to take risks and stand up for truth in the face of moral compromise? Brokenness terrifies us, yet it's the only path to true growth and love of God. It is by assuming a posture of weakness—not to be confused with wimpiness—that we are fully and authentically positioned for usefulness by God. The men in my small group committed to take the plunge—but not alone. We desperately need each other and we need Jesus. He's been there and knows the way.

Like many of you, it is the process of becoming weak, not the result, that scares me. It means dependence on God and reliance on others. It means waiting when I'd rather be running, praying when I'd rather be performing and serving when I'd prefer to be the center of attention. I am a long way from where Joni is in her journey. But I'm getting there, with the help of a Friend who knows my weakness and shares my suffering.

Let me be clear. To be weak and broken does not mean we must become ill, injured or traumatized. It is about posture toward others and toward God. A couple years ago I felt God confronting me about my need for deeper, soul-level relationships with one or two friends. I had sensed that these people moved toward me in friendship—but only to a point. Why? Was I arrogant? Unfriendly? Rude? Did my pride and ego get in the way? I was curious, so I took the risk of taking them out to coffee and asking them. Their comments were similar.

"I'd like you to listen more and talk less in our relationship."

"Sometimes when I'm with you I sense you are not fully present."

"Sometimes I feel like your agenda is more important than mine."

Ouch. These words were delivered in love but landed firmly on my soul. A familiar proverb came to mind: "Wounds from a friend can be trusted" (27:6). Jesus had become a close friend to me, but I had not extended his friendship toward others.

I was broken and saddened. Missed opportunities flashed before my eyes as I pictured moments with these friends when I had controlled the conversation and monopolized the time. I felt shame. No wonder they came no closer; I was holding them at bay with my actions and words—my many words. Another proverb came to mind: "A man of knowledge uses words with restraint" (17:27).

Again I found myself confronted with an opportunity for growth. Would I respond with defensiveness and anger, or with humility? A flood of grace came over me from Jesus, my sacred friend. It was as though he said, "I love you, Bill. So much that I sent these people into your life to expose your faults and inspire your growth. If you remain weak and humble, I will help you in this area. But I need you to be vulnerable and to trust me." I apologized to my friends and owned my foolishness. Immediately I felt embraced by these men and by Jesus, who knows my weaknesses. I was at once free—free to grow and build these relationships.

In this instance, weakness meant taking the posture of a listener and a learner, not a teacher or a teller. These people loved me and reflected the love and truth of God to me. They were also revealing a broken part of me—the need to control, the need to be first, the need to be right. God wanted me to move closer to these people for my sake and theirs. But it meant accepting a level of brokenness, allowing Christ to meet me there with his healing grace.

As hard as it might seem, let us admit our weaknesses to one another and to the One who knows them best. Let us discover freedom, hope and power.

There is no need to hide and pout. The door is open, and it's time to come out. Our sacred friend loves us, and he invites us to the table of community—with all our weaknesses and sin.

Come. There is an open chair waiting, and the place card has your name on it.

❧ PERSONAL RESPONSE

Are you able to embrace the reality that you are broken but you are loved? Is it difficult for you to admit and embrace weakness? Why?

❧ DIALOGUE WITH GOD

Lord, I confess that weakness is exactly that to me—weakness. It is hard for me to find strength in it. Yet a deep part of me knows I must. I need grace and power from you to face my weaknesses and admit they can become tools for transformation in your loving hand. So help me to celebrate them, even when that makes no sense (like right now). I will trust you to

*help me, because you are my friend. This is my prayer, and I know you
hear me. Thanks for listening.*

✣ FURTHER BIBLE READING

2 Corinthians 11:30—12:10

A FRIEND WHO CELEBRATES OUR SUCCESS

*Anyone who has faith in me will do what I have been doing.
He will do even greater things than these.*

For high school seniors, graduate school candidates and job seekers,
spring signals the onslaught of a common, often debilitating disease—acceptance letter anxiety. Wondering whether they have been
admitted to their school of choice or hired by the company they admire, applicants eye their mailboxes with a mixture of curiosity and
trepidation. A fat envelope signals good news and is quickly ripped
open. *Yes! I'm in!* An admission form or a job offer is enclosed, and
the envelope contains all the necessary materials for moving ahead
with the process.

Thin envelopes evoke an entirely different response—sadness,
fear, anger and self-degradation, all accompanied by a sense of
worthlessness that seeps into every cell of the body. These letters
might as well be death notices.

*Thank you, Mr. Johnson, for spending time with us. We have care-
fully reviewed your impressive credentials. Although you are highly
qualified, there were other candidates we felt possessed greater ability to perform in this environment. Of course, we wish we could extend an offer to everyone who meets our standards, but we cannot.*

There are many capable applicants for only a handful of positions. Please know, however, that we wish you success in your future endeavors. Thank you for contacting us.

Rejection. It rocks our world. I remember college students who posted their rejection letters on their doors. The dorm hallways seemed to narrow as the letters accumulated—sometimes there were twenty on one door. For some students it was a kind of subversive therapy, a way of dealing with the overwhelming number of *noes* received. For others it was a way of laughing at themselves in an effort to cover the pain. For a few it was a bid for empathy, each form letter crying out, "Someone important lives here—even if these jerks don't think so!" It was eerie, especially if you were a junior. *So that's what I have to look forward to next year!*

To avoid a spring season of rejection, students seeking admission to elite schools often become intoxicated with the admissions process. The fall term is a battleground as competition for coveted spots heats up. People who have been friends for years find themselves vying for admission to the same schools, and they'll do just about anything to best their rivals.

"Girls in my AP English class accused one another of sabotaging graded presentations by stealing the required reading out of each other's backpacks," divulges prep school student Hannah Friedman in an article in *Newsweek*. "One friend, furious that I had applied to her top choice and predicting that I would be a strong competitor, tried to change my mind for a solid week. 'Connecticut is absolutely horrendous in the winter,' she'd say. . . . I suppose the warped mentality of emphasizing college over friendship arises when one equates self-worth with an acceptance letter."

Hmmm. Looks like Hannah is getting an education, but not the one her parents paid for. Along the way she's accumulated a few graduate-level credits in Life 101. She's discovered that people want you to be successful—as long as you're not more successful than they are.

Not so with Jesus, the one who longs for and celebrates our successes.

> Anyone who has faith in me will do what I have been doing. He will do even greater things than these. (John 14:12)

Greater than you, Jesus? *Yes. I am giving you power to do greater things. Greater love to extend, greater hope to share, greater service to others, greater opportunities for impact on a broken world.*

How wonderfully unusual and life-giving it is when someone genuinely celebrates your success. No feigned admiration or trite endorsements. No forced smiles. No self-righteous grimaces at the suggestion of throwing a party for a prodigal son. Just pure, unadulterated joy at seeing you succeed!

Imagine your boss saying, "I want you to manage even greater resources than I do." Right. Or a professor saying, "I want you to become a better teacher than I am, taking my place at this lectern someday." Sure. Or a pastor saying, "I'm here to empower you to do more ministry more effectively than I ever could." You're kidding, right? Now imagine a friend who is so secure in his identity, so comfortable with his authority, so clear about his own purpose and so wild about your friendship that your success is one of his highest priorities.

No need to imagine. Jesus of Nazareth is such a friend.

On one occasion he sent seventy-two of his followers on an itinerant excursion into the villages surrounding Capernaum in Galilee. From all we can tell the trip was a resounding success. And Jesus was not the least intimidated by their amazing performance. As a matter of fact, it was all he had hoped it would be.

The seventy-two returned with joy and said, "Lord, even the demons submit to us in your name."

He replied, "I saw Satan fall like lightning from heaven." (Luke 10:17-18)

This ragtag group of novices, returning from their first experiences in hand-to-hand combat with the forces of evil, rush to Jesus like a group of schoolboys who just plucked a frog from the jaws of an overly curious cat. Jesus grins from ear to ear and knows this successful outing is only the beginning of a journey into the exciting and turbulent world of ministry. Tremendous opportunity and challenge lie ahead, and he is eager for their success. It's as though he says, "Go ahead, outperform me. I love it!"

Jesus celebrates our success and offers his help at every turn. We don't have to compete with him for a place in the kingdom. He puts our name on his resumé and sends it along to the Father in heaven. With those kinds of credentials, admission is guaranteed, along with a full scholarship.

He says to us, "Here, I give you my life and offer you a place in the kingdom. In addition, I give you the power to do even greater things than I did when I walked the earth. It's all included in the admission packet. No CDs or DVDs to buy, no seminars to attend, no five easy payments of thirty-nine dollars a month. Just my power from above and my presence within."

Success, Jesus-style. Amazing. Just for being a friend.

Imagine. You and I have been commissioned to outperform Jesus—and the whole thing is his idea.

✖ PERSONAL RESPONSE

How does it feel when you think of outperforming the Son of God? Gran-

diose? Arrogant? Exciting? Amazing? How can you realize your humble
status before God yet come to grips with his desire to encourage your success, even if it trumps some of the things Jesus did while on earth?

❧ DIALOGUE WITH GOD

Jesus, I want to be successful—but usually for the wrong motives. The fact
that you champion my success is overwhelming and yet refreshing. I know
in a very real way I can never outperform you—you are God. Yet in a mysterious way you are cheerleading that very thing. I know that anything I
do is because you are at work in me. I really can't do a thing without your
power. I guess that's how it works—I can do greater things now because you
work in me in ways you could not while you were on earth. Now, by the
power of your Spirit, I can do greater things—for your purposes and for
your glory. Wow! This is amazing. And hard for me to fathom. All I can do
is pray and believe—and attempt great things for God, with your help. So
here I go, in Jesus' name.

❧ FURTHER BIBLE READING

Matthew 10

3

Jesus

THE TRUTHFUL REVEALER

❧

Some time ago I was watching a television special about the schemes and techniques used by "psychics" to deceive customers. These scam artists use magnets and strings thin as human hair to move objects across tables. Accomplices rigged with hidden microphones work the crowd before a show to gather information about people who are later offered a "free reading." In some cases, operatives get addresses from the studio audience so that someone can go to their residences, look into the homes and spot specific objects, later to be identified in psychic "visions." *I see a red statue on the mantel above a white fireplace. There are three candles next to the statue. Does this sound familiar to you?* Now that's enough to make anyone cough up a few shekels for future readings.

I was particularly intrigued by the exposé of one particular technique. A customer sits at a small round table. She is interested in contacting someone from her past, a dead relative or friend. As expected, the room is dark and a few candles produce a shadowy backdrop against the velvet curtains that cover the walls. The table is draped with a fringed, floor-length cloth. Strange symbols and objects adorn the room. You get the idea.

Then the psychic enters. She's wearing more jewelry than you would find at Saks Fifth Avenue and a dress that's half pink nightgown, half purple parachute. Speaking in a makeshift foreign accent—part African, part Caribbean and part South Bronx—she contacts the netherworld, searching for wandering relatives. The customer seated at the table is eager to connect with her father.

The psychic begins by describing something about the woman's father—something obtained by the guys with the hidden microphones in the lobby before the appointment.

"I am seeing the name . . . Jake. Or is it Jack?"

"Jack! Yes, Jack! Is he okay?"

"He is walking with someone. . . . No, he's walking with a pet, a dog."

"That's his dog Sparky," the customer says, holding back tears. "He died a year before my father passed away."

"Jack says he has a message for you."

Now, with the woman at her emotional zenith, the psychic grabs a blank slate lying on the table and some chalk. She places the slate on her lap as she looks up to heaven.

"Send us a message, Jack. Give us a sign."

A few moments later she holds up the slate. It reads, "Don't worry about Rita—she is in good hands." Turns out that Rita is the woman's mother, and she has been in the hospital for tests. The woman is beside herself, overcome with relief and incredulity at the same time. We know the information was gathered in the lobby, but how did it find its way onto the blank slate?

Actually, there are two slates. When the psychic places the first one on her lap, out of the direct view of the customer, and looks to heaven, an accomplice, sitting quietly under the shrouded table, carefully exchanges slates. He has been listening carefully and has crafted the message. Soon, "Jack's" message appears on the slate.

Our longing to know more about ourselves combined with a hunger for something more mystical—more spiritual—drives seekers and skeptics alike to bookstores and Internet sites searching for answers. We want an inside track to the mysterious nature and wisdom of God. This inner drive leads many to fortunetellers, psychics and other questionable mediums. We are constantly checking our spiritual e-mail to see if there are any messages from God. That's where Jesus comes in.

Jesus had a message from God. Better yet, he *was* the message from God. Instead of using hidden microphones or sleight of hand, he told people to watch, look and listen. He had become the living Word—the message—and had come to reveal mysteries about us, about God, about the world and about the future.

Jesus is a truthful revealer, a messenger from God with words for a world in which there are many questions and few clear answers.

THE REVEALER WHO DESCRIBES OUR FATHER

Anyone who has seen me has seen the Father.

What was your dad like? Is he still alive? What did you enjoy most about him? What are your earliest memories?

I am sure many images flood your mind when you're asked about your father.

As a young man my father was strong and active. I remember riding on his broad shoulders, or wrapping my arms around them as I hitched a ride on his back in the swimming pool where he worked every summer. Though now retired, he taught high school physical education and health classes for about thirty-five years, and he coached swimming and cross-country teams. As I grew up I came to admire my dad's courage and his love for people. If there was an automobile accident in the area, he went to help. When a student needed a ride home after practice, he tried to accommodate the request.

One evening when I was about thirteen, my mother came home upset and crying. She had been out shopping and it was 9 p.m. "A man is after me! All the way home from the store he followed me in his car!" No sooner did those words leave her lips than my dad shifted into attack mode, heading out the door like a tiger chasing prey. I had never seen him act that way before. But I knew one thing; if that guy was within reach, he was going to wish he'd stayed in the frozen food aisle.

Over the years I saw many sides of my dad. I watched him show kindness to the elderly and make kids laugh. He often worked three jobs—teaching, coaching and officiating at sports events—just to provide for us. He was a defender of the weak and never afraid to confront the unruly. Once we attended a Philadelphia Phillies baseball game, a rare treat because of the cost. In about the third inning some mildly inebriated men seated about five rows behind us began to shout profanity at the players. A steady flow of four-letter words cascaded over our heads. Dad did not spend his hard-earned money to listen to this verbal barrage the entire game. At first he shot a disgusted glance their way. It had no impact; the words continued. So he turned to give an angry, lingering look, hoping that would do the trick. More words. Then Dad asked them to stop. This time the cuss words were accompanied by laughter. Not smart. At this point Dad stood up and turned around.

At first I was embarrassed. My dad, who was six-foot-two and weighed 265 pounds, attracted the attention of several rows of people in our vicinity. But quickly my chagrin turned to admiration. Here was my dad, confronting three or four loudmouthed drunks who were ruining the game for everyone within twenty feet. The security guards had done nothing. The people around the drunks had done nothing. Not my dad. He wasn't a do-nothing kind of guy.

My dad pointed his finger at the thugs and spoke firmly and deliberately. I forget the exact words, though his comments included something like, "And if I hear any more, I'm going to personally come up there and help you stop." They decided not to take Dad up on his offer and we all enjoyed the rest of the game.

My dad was strong and confident, a hard worker. He was our protector and provider. He always loved his family (he still does) and sacrificed to make our lives better.

Images of our earthly fathers help us form a rough sketch for the picture we hold of our heavenly Father. The words "heavenly Father" may provoke a negative or scornful reaction in those whose earthly fathers left much to be desired. Abusive, distant, demanding or controlling fathers leave many with a warped sense of fatherhood, one often superimposed over their image of God.

The 1996 pop song "Counting Blue Cars" by the group Dishwalla rejects the male language commonly used to describe God in biblical writings. The song portrays a curious child who wonders what it would be like to meet God—to meet *her*—face to face. Around the same time, Joan Osborne's album *Relish* was released and included a song that questioned whether God was just a regular "slob" like you and me, or like your average stranger riding the bus to work. What if God was really like that? How do we know? Or what if God is just an idea or a tree, or a force or a rabbit or a cosmic energy or a soul wind? Our misperceptions of what God should be like may hinder us from encountering him as he really is.

Missing persons report: Old man, five-foot-nine and weighing about 175 pounds. Shoulder-length, graying hair and full beard. Walks slowly, looks kindly and is somewhat fragile. Often seen in the park handing out goodies. Calm disposition. Not easily angered. Highly tolerant. Enjoys sitting in large, comfortable chairs. Please let us know if you have seen him. Answers to the name "God."

Do we have a heavenly Father or a heavenly concept? Our impression of God may have no basis in fact; it may simply be a conglomeration of perceptions and experiences. And our impression shapes the way we think about him and relate to him—until we encounter Jesus.

Jesus came to reveal the Father. "No one has ever seen God, but God the One and Only, who is at the Father's side, has made him known" (John 1:18). This God who is at the Father's side is Jesus. And he came in the flesh to show us the Father. But we must look carefully at him—lest we superimpose our preconceived father-image onto Jesus.

> Philip said, "Lord, show us the Father and that will be enough for us."
>
> Jesus answered: "Don't you know me, Philip, even after I have been among you such a long time? Anyone who has seen me has seen the Father." (John 14:8-9)

"Like father, like son," the old saying goes. If that's true, and Jesus' words are true, then we have more than a sketch or concept of God—

we have a living portrait. And on close examination we see that he is strong but not oppressive, loving but not smothering, kind but not wimpy, loyal but not clingy, truthful but not harsh, forceful but never abusive, caring and yet not intrusive.

Jesus had such a relationship with the Father in heaven. He called his Father *Abba*, an affectionate and intimate term akin to "daddy." Children of all ages need a heavenly daddy. Jesus shows us the kind of father who would spend a day with you fishing or walking in the park or hanging out at the art museum, but who also can fend off evil and stand for justice. A gentle, courageous friend. A powerful and loving dad.

So tell me, what's your heavenly Father like? If there's any confusion, look at Jesus, who says, "When a man believes in me, he does not believe in me only, but in the one who sent me. When he looks at me, he sees the one who sent me" (John 12:44-45).

✤ PERSONAL RESPONSE

How has your experience with your earthly father affected your image of your heavenly Father? How does it feel to call God "Daddy," as Jesus did?

✤ DIALOGUE WITH GOD

Jesus, show me my heavenly Father. Help me to see him in your actions and your words, your feelings and thoughts, your loving deeds and courageous exploits. I want to know him deeply and see him fully, so I am looking squarely at you. Remove my blindness and destroy my idols. I want to see you as you really are. Help me, I pray.

✤ FURTHER BIBLE READING

John 14

The Revealer Who Discloses Our Identity

He calls his own sheep by name.

At age eighteen he became the world's youngest commercial airline pilot; in the same year he was named head of the pediatrics unit at a hospital; at nineteen he passed the bar exam and became a licensed attorney. The world's smartest man? No—the world's most famous liar. Frank Abagnale, whose true life story was depicted in the movie *Catch Me If You Can,* writes in his autobiography by the same title that he lived a life full of falsified documents, fake ID cards and phony checks. He could change his name or his career, but never his true identity.

Who are we . . . really? Only God knows . . . really.

Their given names were Simon, James and John, and they were fishermen by trade. But who were they? What did Jesus see in them that others did not? No sensible rabbi trying to launch a worldwide movement would choose this rabble for his inner circle. They and their companions were mostly unlearned men, great with a net but unskilled in politics, religion and culture. This was an unwieldy group for Jesus, and leading them was like herding cats. What was he thinking? Who was he after?

Wanted: twelve unstable men with little experience in foreign affairs to accompany rabbi on three-year road trip. Destination undisclosed. Must be willing to leave family for extended periods of time. No formal education needed. No salary, no offices, no supplies provided. No transportation offered. Extra clothing or money not permitted. Job description: fishing for people and unconditionally following the rabbi. Housing: hopefully. Failure: often. Persecution: almost certainly. Upon completion of the mission you will receive the

same reward as Old Testament prophets received. Call 1-800-DIE-
2DAY to schedule an interview.

Look at Simon. He was an impulsive idealist whose motto was "shoot, ready, aim." His method of operation? First in, first out. First into the water, first out of the boat. First into the conversation, first to lose touch with reality. First to identify Jesus as the Messiah, first to deny knowing him.

But Jesus knew Simon's real identity. He saw past the fisherman's surface idealism and found a bold visionary within. So Jesus decided to designate him the first leader of his church. To prove the point he changed Simon's name, revealing a newer—and truer—identity.

Blessed are you, Simon son of Jonah, for this was not revealed
to you by man, but by my Father in heaven. And I tell you that
you are Peter, and on this rock I will build my church, and the
gates of Hades will not overcome it. (Matthew 16:17-18)

Jesus referred to Peter as a strong rock, a bedrock, a sure foundation on which all the church would grow in strength. He revealed Peter's true identity as a rock because he knew God was going to use Peter and his faith to build something great—a new community. Peter understood this more fully as he matured in his teaching, calling all Christ-followers "living stones" that "are being built into a spiritual house" (1 Peter 2:5). This enthusiastic fisherman had discovered his true identity—and it changed the trajectory of his life forever.

Then there were James and John, sons of Zebedee. At least that's how most people knew them. Jesus experienced them much differently. These two were agitators in the community, often stirring the pot of controversy with their caustic words and selfish ambitions.

One day, just after Jesus explained that the least in the kingdom would actually be the greatest, James and John approached him, along with their mother, and asked if they could have the seats of privilege next to Jesus when he set up his kingdom. Like today's Beltway insiders in Washington, they wanted to be headquartered near the Oval Office, at the nucleus of power and influence. And they used their mom to lobby Jesus because she was an ardent supporter of his work (probably financially or by cooking meals). I can hear her now, the quintessential Jewish mother.

"You know, Jesus, how much I love your work. And I've given you these sons of mine, two fine Jewish boys to help. So I wonder if you could do something for us. You see, I was hoping that James would be a doctor and John an attorney, but instead they left everything behind—including graduate school—to follow you. Oy, I'm telling you, boys can break a mother's heart. So I'm asking a small favor. Go ahead, boys, ask him."

"Uh, Jesus . . . Mom wants to know if we can sit next to you in heaven."

When the others heard about the deal James and John were trying to cut, the Bible says they became "indignant" (Matthew 20:24), which is a nice way of saying they went ballistic. Who were these guys to shove their way to the top?

And what of the time that James and John decided to become Jesus' avengers? In Luke 9 the leaders in a Samaritan village refused to welcome the disciples who had been sent there ahead of Jesus to prepare for his arrival. The Samaritans—who hated the Jews as much as the Jews despised them—had heard that Jesus was heading to Jerusalem, the focal point for the Jewish faith, and they wanted nothing to do with him. So James and John, acting as loving and forgiving Christ-followers, asked Jesus, "Lord, do you want us to call fire down from heaven to destroy them?" (Luke 9:54). Jesus rebuked them and headed to another village instead. Can you imagine Jesus' frustration? No wonder he nicknamed them "Sons of Thunder." They were activist agitators, kicking up dust and disagreements almost everywhere they went.

But over time, Jesus got hold of their hearts and transformed them, giving them a newer and truer identity. These sons of thunder—these agitators turned initiators—would eventually rock the world. Let's fast-forward a few years. James must have caused some damage for the kingdom of heaven, because he became one of the church's first martyrs, dying at the hands of Herod Agrippa I around A.D. 40. He certainly had to be a prominent and effective leader to warrant that kind of attention.

As for John, he gives us some of the greatest literature the world has ever read, revealing the great mysteries of God and his irrational, relentless love for people. In his Gospel and three New Testament letters, John refers to "love" well over one hundred times, more than any other New Testament writer. Only the poetic literature of the Old Testament—mostly the Psalms, Proverbs and Song of Solomon—exceeds the use of the term. Amazing. This would-be terminator, who wanted to incinerate an entire city, had become the apostle of love.

There's another disciple who discovered his true identity when he met the truthful revealer—me. When I encountered Jesus I was an entertainer of sorts, the life of the party and center of attention. I enjoyed making people laugh. It felt good inside. My relationships reflected that persona. Sometimes that humor and energy were misdirected, coming out in crude jokes, racial slurs and inappropriate comments about women. But it got me some laughs and I felt good about the attention.

Thankfully, God had bigger and better plans for me. As I began to follow this Jesus and seek his ways, I remember feeling intensely loved for who I was, not simply how I performed. Christ began to reveal my identity—I was a child of the King, a beloved creation, a man made for serving people and enjoying God's gracious gifts. I also discovered I had the ability to teach. I began to enjoy not simply entertaining people, but guiding them into the provocative and life-giving teachings of Jesus. And he affirmed my love of humor, though he also revealed how I used it at times to hide my insecurities or mask my pain.

Jesus affirmed my introverted side as well. (I am half-extrovert, half-introvert. One half loves a good party; the other half wants to sit alone and read for two days afterward.) The introvert in me loves to study and write; the extrovert enjoys public speaking and a rich experience in community with others. God has allowed me to live a life that honors both parts of me.

We all have two identities—one surface, one hidden. Jesus can transform us and call out that hidden, truer identity. As a young con artist, Frank Abagnale was a master at the career-changing business, but that's surface transformation. Jesus is in the identity-changing business. And that goes down to the core, deep into our spiritual DNA. In the company of Jesus, agitators become initiators, idealists become visionaries, terminators become lovers.

And insecure clowns can become confident communicators of his love and goodness. I'm still amazed.

Discovering our inner identity requires humility, a setting aside of the falsified documents and fake ID card we have been carrying around, exchanging them for the authentic life Jesus created. The choice is ours. Like a toddler we can cling to the security blanket of our old identity. But is it really that secure? Even a frightened toddler rushes to the arms of mom or dad, not to a blanket. It's time to let go of the false self and ask God to change us—from the inside out. And he will. He will give us a new name.

✿ PERSONAL RESPONSE

How many times do you find yourself living up to others' expectations of who you should be? What will it take for you to get a reality check, look at yourself and claim your God-given identity?

✿ DIALOGUE WITH GOD

God, who am I really? A leader, a follower? A child loved by you? Or am I a master of disguise? A phony? Am I a true friend or someone watching out for numero uno? Sometimes it's hard to tell. So I know I must derive my true identity from you—not from the world or my own imagination. Because I choose to follow you I know I have a new name, a new identity in Christ. I need you to shape and mold that identity, discarding the false self I have manufactured for protection and safety. Thanks for showing me who I can really be. Thanks for making me yours.

✿ FURTHER BIBLE READING

Ephesians 1

THE REVEALER WHO UNCOVERS OUR PAST

He told me everything I ever did.

If sales of the Left Behind series are any indication (sixty-two million at this writing), Americans—particularly Christians—are obsessed with the future. We love to envision a preferred future, even though we fret about the quality of life that lies ahead. Will we die young, retire healthy, be financially sound, see our grandchildren, lose our jobs, keep our hair (or is that keep our jobs, lose our hair?), find a spouse, stay happily married and so on? The future is mysterious and open-ended, ensuring job security for part-time prophets and palm readers alike.

But perhaps our preoccupation with the future keeps us from facing our past, which many of us would rather forget. After all, we can't change it, so why worry? Get over it. Let bygones be bygones.

This is easier for some than others. In 1993 Mende Nazer was kidnapped at age twelve from her Sudanese village and sold as a slave to an Arab family in Khartoum. For seven horrifying years she was beaten and sexually abused. At one point she was burned with a hot ladle for serving fried eggs instead of poached. She finally escaped and is now able to tell the chilling tale in her autobiography *Slave: My True Story*. She has no desire to run from or hide her past because the past is part of who she is and a means for helping others who are subject to the same cruelty.

God is interested in the past as much as he is the present and future. When Jesus met a woman at a well in Samaria, he uncovered her sordid, promiscuous past. Not to make himself feel superior, to shame her or to satisfy the curiosity of onlookers. He did so for her benefit so that when she faced her past, she could embrace the present with joy and step freely into the future with hope. John 4 describes the account—and you need to read it in full. But in a nutshell, here's what happened.

Jesus stopped for water at Jacob's well on the outskirts of Sychar, a village in Samaria, on his way to Jerusalem. His disciples had entered the village to buy food, though Jews and Samaritans deeply despised one another. Certainly they were hoping this would be a quick stopover. But that didn't keep Jesus from seeking a drink from a Samaritan woman's cup. She was the epitome of everything a Jewish rabbi would avoid at all costs. She was a woman, she lived in Samaria (enemy territory), she'd had five marriages and was sleeping with a man who wasn't her husband, and she was alone. Not someone you'd want to brag about meeting at the next synagogue gathering. All she needed was "Turn and run!" printed on her forehead.

But Jesus broke all the rules of etiquette—he talked to her, sat with her and drank from her cup. He used this interaction as a metaphor for the spiritual life he longed to give her. She had come to a well with a bucket because she had no water—he had no bucket but offered to draw living water from a spiritual well. The irony is overwhelming. But there was one big hurdle—her past.

> "Go call your husband and then come back."
>
> "I have no husband," she said.
>
> "That's nicely put: 'I have no husband.' You've had five husbands, and the man you're living with now isn't even your husband. You spoke the truth there, sure enough." (John 4:16-18 *The Message*)

Eventually Jesus revealed that he was the Messiah whom Samaritans and Jews were both seeking, and the woman ran and told the entire village. Many found her words to be true, believed and followed Jesus. It's an amazing story. It's probably a good thing the disciples weren't there. One look at this woman's resumé and they'd have never left Jesus alone with her, probably urging him to leave.

But let's roll the tape back to the part about the husbands. Why bring it up? Why didn't Jesus simply describe his offer of life and his identity as the Christ? Even though he shocked her by revealing her less than wonderful past, she neither repented nor cowered in shame. Instead she changed the subject. Why bother to dig up her sin-stained history?

If we read between the lines, it's clear that when Jesus uncovered her past and disclosed his identity, she experienced grace and found hope. "He told me everything I ever did!" she exclaimed (John 4:39). You just don't go running around shouting about your past if you're this woman—even if the whole village already knows it. That's probably why she was at the well in the heat of the day instead of the cool of the morning or evening when other women came. Everyone knew her lifestyle, and she was likely the frequent object of scorn and derision. Only one thing could change her from a conniving temptress to a compelling evangelist—the matchless love of Jesus. This was her day with Messiah. Her day to face her past and run from it into the freeing grace of God.

Like Mende Nazer, the Samaritan woman used her past to change someone else's present. Both had tragic histories. Both found freedom. And then, using the past they wished had never been, both made freedom possible for others.

> But when the time arrived that was set by God the Father, God sent his Son, born among us of a woman, born under the conditions of the law so that he might redeem those of us who have been kidnapped by the law. (Galatians 4:4 *The Message*)

The future looks bright when you face the past, no matter how ugly or broken it may be. When God uncovers and reveals our past— the full impact of our sin, the tragic consequences of our pain—it is for a purpose. To guide us to the only one who can unlock the shackles that enslave us.

PERSONAL RESPONSE

Look at your past. What do you see? What do you think God sees? And how might God redeem your past?

❧ DIALOGUE WITH GOD

Jesus, meet me like you did the woman at the well. Show me my past and help me see that despite how bad it is, I can find new life in you. Freedom, joy and hope are hidden there, waiting to be unlocked by your unyielding love. Grant me the courage to face the dark realities of my sinful past so that I can embrace the glorious reality of a wonderful future in your presence. I need that today. And if in some way my past can become a doorway to freedom in someone else's future, use it to your glory, I pray, in the name of Christ, the Messiah.

❧ FURTHER BIBLE READING

Romans 6

THE REVEALER WHO EXPOSES OUR NEEDS

[Jesus] came to seek and to save what was lost.

Derrick Adkins would never be on someone's "needy" list. In 1996 in Atlanta he won the 400-meter hurdles to capture an Olympic gold medal. It was supposed to be the greatest moment of his life—but soon afterward he retreated into a state of depression. Derrick had first experienced depression at the age of thirteen, but running track helped distract him from his problem and he pursued athletics rigorously. Soon he became the greatest hurdler in America, but he struggled once again with discontentment. Happiness eluded him, though he always felt it was within his grasp. "Once I get to college, I'll be happy," he told himself. Then it became, "If I can be the nation's best collegiate hurdler, I'll be happy." Then, "Once I get a new car, I'll be happy." "Once I buy a house, I'll be happy."

Derrick discovered that nothing made him happy—not money, not drinking, not training, not self-help books. Six months before the Atlanta games he had been diagnosed as a chronic depressive and was given Luvox, an antidepressant, but it made him tired so he stopped taking it—he was training for the gold. Finally, after returning from a trip to Europe after his victory at the Olympics, he admitted his need and began taking the medication again. "Guess what? I've been doing well ever since," he says. Derrick admits, "I didn't want to be labeled a chronic depressive, a mental patient, a crazy person. As it turned out, my pride caused me a lot of pain."

Each of us has a chronic disease—one that pride keeps us from addressing. The Bible calls it sin. We'd rather not call it that. We'd rather use terms like "an error in judgment" or "some mistakes" or "a small miscalculation"—anything but sin. Sin means we miss the mark, which indicates we come nowhere near the target God has set for a right relationship with him. We all have the disease, and we all commit acts of sin as a result. If you don't believe this happens to you, just ask someone close to you—they'll fill you in. Truthfully, we all need help, and self-help won't work. Like Derrick, we need something we don't have within us. And we have to give up something to get it.

"Since I've been medicated," Derrick laments, "my track career hasn't been the same. The fatigue has proved too severe for me to run with the world's best. I now accept the fact that my health is more important than winning races." I think there's a spiritual corollary here. Maybe we need to give up "winning races" in order to get spiritually healthy. Maybe what we need is something the world can't provide. Closing another deal, making another sale, winning another trophy just won't cut it any more. As Derrick confides after all his success, "Still I felt something was missing."

We need to find a better way. We need someone to rescue us from ourselves so that we can find a cure for the pain of separation between us and God. Jesus can bridge that gap and restore the relationship. Jesus exposes our need for grace, forgiveness and reconciliation—then he meets that need by giving us his life. The only thing standing in the way is the same thing that stopped a young Olympian from seeking the help he needed—pride. Fear of exposure was Adkins's greatest hurdle. To leap over this one he needed help. And when he accepted that fact, it made all the difference in the world.

"I finally have peace and joy, two things far greater than an Olympic gold medal," he says. "I've found that praying and reading Scriptures helps me stay balanced emotionally; therefore, I've entered theology school and will dedicate the rest of my life to inspiring others." Derrick seems to have found his way.

Some of us need affection or attention; some of us need truth and grace; but we all need help. And God offers help for the spiritual and emotional cravings that characterize our souls. But first we must admit we need him. And like Derrick, we will find our way. In his case, it included a new adventure in theology school. But it's different for us—as plumbers, teachers, businesswomen or short-order cooks. We find our way in the midst of our vocation. Our work and relationships take on new meaning when we encounter Jesus as the truthful revealer who exposes our need for grace and peace.

"I'm a man with a mission and a message," says Derrick Adkins. "Don't be too proud to seek help, and remember that all that glitters ain't gold."

Jesus, [discussing who is worthy of an invitation to the kingdom, said to his critics,] "Who needs a doctor: the healthy or the sick? I'm here inviting the sin-sick, not the spiritually fit." (Mark 2:17 *The Message*)

If you recognize that you are needy—if you require medication for the disease called sin—the doctor will see you now.

✸ PERSONAL RESPONSE

What are you chasing that you hope will bring you happiness? How would someone who really knows you complete this sentence for you: "As soon as I _____, then I will be happy"?

✸ DIALOGUE WITH GOD

Dear God, who am I kidding? I am sick. I need the Great Physician to examine me, expose the disease and bring the cure. It may be painful and I know it will require letting go of some things that I think will bring me joy. Stuff I cling to, trophies I long to have on my shelf, accomplishments that make me feel bigger and stronger and faster than others running the race of life. But I'm ready now—especially if it means spiritual health. I still feel that something's missing. So do your work in me. That's all I ask.

✸ FURTHER BIBLE READING

Romans 3:9-26

THE REVEALER WHO UNVEILS OUR DESTINY

I am going . . . to prepare a place for you.

Family vacations can be exhilarating or exhausting—or both. Christmas 1993 was a vacation that would live in infamy in our family. Just a year after moving to Chicago from Dallas, we decided to join Gail's family in San Antonio for the holidays. A stop in Dallas seemed like a natural addition to the itinerary since we had so many friends there.

We had met, married and had our first child, Ryan, in "the Big D." He was now four years old. Unfortunately, things did not turn out as expected. In a Christmas letter to friends and family, we recounted the experience in poetry.

'Twas the week before Christmas and we decided to travel,
but before we could get there the trip would unravel.
Though our baggage was checked by a nice clerk name Alice,
Half went to El Paso, half joined us in Dallas.

We gathered together to ponder our sorrow
But the airline assured us "You'll get it tomorrow!"
We readied ourselves amidst all the clatter
But suddenly something else was the matter.

We'd borrowed a home to cut travel cost,
But the security code that we needed was lost.
After some panic we realized the mistake—
The code was at home back in ole Crystal Lake.

So we made some calls to the neighbor's abode
And she hunted and found the security code.
Finally from the airport we headed with glee,
With half of our luggage, the code and a key.

On the way we stopped at our restaurant of choice
But during the dinner, Gail lost her voice.
The cough she'd been fighting had turned for the worst
And we began to believe our vacation was cursed.

We seriously questioned this trip we were making,
especially when Ryan's ear started aching.
We got ourselves all snuggled up in our beds,

While visions of doctor bills danced in our heads.

Our luggage arrived the next day as expected
But Gail's voice was now gone and Ryan's ear was infected.
The day was filled with appointments—booked solid;
But on the way to a friend's home, Bill lost his wallet.

Later we found it, so don't be disturbed;
It lay in a puddle on the road near the curb.
After four days in Dallas and a trip to the doc,
We headed to San Antonio for our last Christmas stop.

The time there was restful and we all soon recovered,
Until our plane tickets could not be discovered.
So I in my kerchief and Ma in her cap
Pleaded with the airline to let us fly back.

"If you repurchase your tickets you can fly in a pinch!"
said the nice ticket agent who resembled the Grinch.
So with tickets and bags and wallet and voice,
We flew back to Chicago, our city of choice.

Though the weather reminded us of Anchorage and Gnome,
We decided (like Dorothy) there's no place like home!

Whenever people prepare to travel to new destinations, there are many questions. *Will the condo look like the picture on the Internet? What will the weather be like? Will the kids like it? Are the directions accurate? What will we do after we get there? Does everyone have enough clean underwear?*

In the spiritual realm the questions are similar but far more significant. *Where is my life going? How will it end? What is heaven like? Are the descriptions in the Bible symbolic or literal? Is it a place or an experi-*

ence? Will I like it? Who else will be there? And what will I wear? (Yes, I've heard someone ask that.) We want life to be an adventure but we all ultimately want to know where the adventure is taking us.

Jesus left little doubt. Here are a few things he said about our destiny.

I tell you the truth, whoever hears my word and believes him who sent me has eternal life and will not be condemned; he has crossed over from death to life. (John 5:24)

No one knows about that day or hour, not even the angels in heaven, nor the Son, but only the Father. Be on guard! Be alert! You do not know when that time will come. It's like a man going away: He leaves his house and puts his servants in charge, each with his assigned task, and tells the one at the door to keep watch.

Therefore keep watch because you do not know when the owner of the house will come back—whether in the evening, or at midnight, or when the rooster crows, or at dawn. If he comes suddenly, do not let him find you sleeping. What I say to you, I say to everyone: "Watch!" (Mark 13:32-37)

Do not let your hearts be troubled. Trust in God; trust also in me. In my Father's house are many rooms; if it were not so, I would have told you. I am going there to prepare a place for you. And if I go and prepare a place for you, I will come back and take you to be with me that you also may be where I am. (John 14:1-3)

Heaven begins here, where our Jesus-life is. "The kingdom of heaven is near," Christ said (Matthew 10:7). Heaven begins when we say, "I want the life Jesus is talking about." Like marriage, heaven is more about a person than a place. A wedding is an event—a marriage is a relationship. Heaven begins with an event—a transformational encounter with Jesus. But that relationship is eternal.

Our destiny is a person, not a place. And our relationship with that person includes great activity, wonder and joy. It is fresh and new, unlike anything we've read about or seen. We get a glimpse of it now because we have an experience with God and his people now. Full disclosure awaits for when we will say, like John, "I saw a new heaven and a new earth" (Revelation 21:1).

We will share in the reign over this new heaven and earth, this new environment Jesus is shaping so that we might be forever in his company.

> The Throne of God and of the Lamb is at the center. His servants will offer God service—worshiping, they'll look on his face, their foreheads mirroring God. Never again will there be any night. No one will need lamplight or sunlight. The shining of God, the Master, is all the light anyone needs. And they will rule with him age after age after age. (Revelation 22:3-5 *The Message*)

No tears, no pain, no darkness of soul or spirit. No depression or anxiety, no ADHD, no cancer, no AIDS, no suffering, no disabilities or "challenges," no death. Just pure, unrivaled joy with God and his family, sharing the fullness of a life filled with true intimacy and invigorating activity, unfettered and without shame or guilt.

Sounds like the family vacation we always wanted.

❧ PERSONAL RESPONSE

God has shown his followers their ultimate destiny—one that begins here and leads into eternity. Where are you on the journey? Still holding back from following? Or are you sure of your destiny but never thought that your future actually begins today?

❧ DIALOGUE WITH GOD

God, some days I just want to go home. But then I remember the people I know and the kids I care for and the spouse I love. And I see the work that there is to do. Help me to be a faithful traveler on the road you have paved before me. I want to travel with my eyes fixed on the hope I have in Christ and my mind alert to the opportunities to serve him and others here and now. Help me to travel well, because I know that my destiny is secure. This is my prayer and desire.

❧ FURTHER BIBLE READING

1 Peter 1:1-12

4

Jesus

THE EXTREME FORGIVER

❧

Nelson Mandela ranks near the top of the list of modern-day extreme forgivers. After twenty-seven years of unjust and abusive imprisonment in South Africa, Mandela emerged a hero—a hero with many options.

He was the leader of the African National Congress, the prevailing political party formed in the 1940s to bring reform to the country. His people had been oppressed for many years by a foreign white regime, the Dutch Afrikaans National Party, which passed laws to place blacks in "native" settlement areas. This policy of separation was formalized and institutionalized as apartheid ("apartness"). The Afrikaans leadership asserted, *Die wit man moet altyd baas wees* ("The white man must always remain boss"). Under this oppressive regime, Mandela, a lawyer and political leader, was charged with treason and ultimately imprisoned.

In prison Mandela suffered mistreatment and humiliation, which he describes in his autobiography *Long Walk to Freedom*. On one occasion he was transferred in the back of a van for about ten hours, shackled to four prisoners with only a sanitary bucket to use. "It is not an easy or pleasant task for men shackled together to use a sanitary bucket in a moving van," he writes. What an understatement. Upon arrival at prison they were stripped of their clothes in a room filled with two inches of water. Their clothes were thrown onto the floor; the men were inspected and then told to dress in the wet clothes.

"The authorities," he continues, "liked to say we received a balanced diet; it was indeed balanced—between the unpalatable and the inedible." "Coffee" was actually ground maize, baked until black and combined with hot water. The bathing and drinking water was brackish, and days were spent hammering rocks and doing hard labor. Often blacks were forced to wear shorts because the authorities wanted them to feel like boys, not men. Mandela protested vigorously and received a pair of long pants—along with a month in solitary confinement.

> I did not see the face or hear the voice of another prisoner. I was locked up for twenty-three hours a day, with thirty minutes of exercise in the morning and again in the afternoon. . . . There was no natural light in my cell; a single bulb burned overhead twenty-four hours a day. . . . I had nothing to read, nothing to write on or with, no one to talk to. The mind begins to turn in on itself, and one desperately wants something outside of oneself on which to fix one's attention. I have known men who have taken half-a-dozen lashes in preference to being locked up alone. After a time in solitary, I relished the company even of the insects in my cell, and found myself on the verge of initiating conversations with a cockroach. . . . Nothing is more dehumanizing than the absence of human companionship.

Despite the harshness, Mandela was spared the worst because of the national exposure his imprisonment provoked. Others were less fortunate, facing the full brunt of brutality and humiliation.

During his imprisonment Mandela was mostly separated from his wife, Winnie, and family, and his people were forcibly moved into townships outside the cities, where there was no plumbing or electricity except for the surveillance lamps high above the streets so helicopters could track criminals at night. There was no education; no one could drive a car. Men had to take buses and taxis to work in menial jobs. Medical clinics were few and ill-equipped, food was scarce, and disease ran rampant.

Put yourself in Mandela's shoes. You have just emerged from prison, freed after twenty-seven years of injustice, and your political party is strong. Blacks have been elected to power. Of the forty million people in your country, only 10 percent are white, and these Dutch and British people oppressed you for decades. Your people are angry and destitute. The white government has squandered your natural resources and mismanaged the funds, handing back a debt-ridden economy on the verge of bankruptcy. What do you do?

Do you incite the angry mobs and hostile youth to rise up? Or do you turn the economic tables, forcing whites from their wealthy homes and making them live in squatter camps? Or do you simply evict the whites from the country, even the few who rallied to your cause? After all, this is your land. You are seventy-one, having entered prison at age forty-four, sacrificing the prime of your life for a cause you believed in. Do you spend your remaining years recounting your ordeal and using it as a political weapon to achieve your own ends?

Nelson Mandela chose none of this. Somehow he was able to continue his fight for a unified Africa and yet not resent his oppressors. "I was asked about the fears of whites. I knew people expected me to harbor anger toward whites. But I had none. In prison, my anger toward whites decreased, but my hatred for the system grew. I wanted South Africa to see that I loved even my enemies while I hated the system that turned us against one another."

Lewis Smedes, in arguing that we should forgive even those monstrous people who commit atrocities, puts it this way: "The truth of the matter is: very ordinary people do extraordinary evil. We need to judge them, surely, and forgive them, if we can, because they are responsible. And because we need to be healed." To equate even the most despicable person with evil embodied—with Satan—is to dehumanize that person. Only Satan, argues Smedes, is unforgivable because he is pure, nonhuman evil. If we treat humans in this way, it removes responsibility from their actions, for now they are nonhuman and thus not accountable. To forgive is to acknowledge their humanity. Or as Henri Nouwen often remarked, "Forgiveness is allowing the other person not to be God." That is, allowing him or her to be human.

Jesus of Nazareth set the standard for extreme forgiveness. Mistreated, tortured, humiliated, mocked and rejected, he uttered the most remarkable words human ears have ever heard. In his moment of greatest agony he cried, "Father, forgive them, for they do not know what they are doing" (Luke 23:34).

The words are remarkable for several reasons. Jesus is innocent—even Pilate acknowledged he had committed no crime. He was unjustly tried and sentenced, the victim of false accusers and trumped-up charges. He had the power to destroy those who were crucifying him. His death brought his immediate family only grief and shame.

We all took part in the act of crucifying Jesus. His forgiveness was not directed at a few soldiers and religious leaders; it was—and is—offered to the whole world.

Now that's extreme forgiveness.

THE FORGIVER WHO HEARS OUR CONFESSION

Go away from me, Lord; I am a sinful man!

Bill Wilson, the cofounder of Alcoholics Anonymous, was convinced that an alcoholic had to "hit bottom" in order to recover from his addiction. Wilson wrote, "How privileged we are to understand so well the divine paradox that strength rises from weakness, that humiliation goes before resurrection: that pain is not only the price but the very touchstone of spiritual rebirth." An alcoholic must confess—that is, agree—that he or she has an unsolvable problem and is beyond hope for recovery apart from outside help. The beauty of AA is that every week, in tens of thousands of groups around the world, such confessions are readily heard and received, without judgment, shame or incredulity.

It is the possibility of mercy, not the fear of retribution, that moves people to genuine confession. A coerced confession is rarely truthful, as people will say anything to escape the threat of pain or judgment. Indeed, lying may delay wrath, but only a sincere confession can evoke mercy.

We experience soul-level freedom every time we admit brokenness, despair and failure in the company of grace-filled mercy-givers. And confessions come easily when wrongdoers are assured of the gracious and merciful response of the one offended.

Do you . . . not realiz[e] that God's kindness leads you toward repentance? (Romans 2:4)

I studied at the University of North Texas for my Ph.D., so I ventured onto the campus several days a month for classes and library research. One day, while crossing the courtyard outside the student center, I heard—and then saw—a man screaming at a group of students. Some were seated on the concrete benches along the perimeter of the square while others sat on the ground, alone or huddled in groups. It was the lunch hour and this was a favorite gathering place to connect with friends and roommates at midday.

It soon became apparent that this man was an angry preacher. He was laying into these college students with a ferocity that I had not seen in many years. Reactions from the small crowd of about thirty were mixed. Some ignored him, some laughed and mocked him, and some appeared angry. But one thing was certain; he was taking no prisoners. His tone was harsh, his mannerisms wooden, his face contorted with rage and his message venomous. "You drunkards and fornicators," he railed. "Do you think you can hide from God? Do you think he doesn't see everything you do in those dormitory rooms at night? The parties, the sex, the drugs?"

Suddenly, my adrenaline kicked in and I found myself standing beside the preacher. Believe me, we were both shocked. I had no prepared message, but I did have something he didn't—the undivided attention of thirty college students. I was angry at his distorted portrayal of truth and sad for these open-minded, truth-seeking students who might never get a glimpse of the real Jesus.

I poured out my heart to these young people, describing the relentless love of God shown to them in Christ, how they mattered to him and how his greatest pleasure would be to become friends with them. I acknowledged that God was holy and that sin destroyed relationships and drove a wedge between us and a loving Creator. But then I spoke of life and hope, forgiveness and freedom.

And then I stepped down, wondering if I had just made a total fool of myself. Feeling awkward and a bit embarrassed at the whole spectacle, I cut a circuitous route away from the crowd toward my classroom. A student pursued me and asked if we could talk. The look in his eyes told me this was not going to be about the weather or some finer point of theology. Class would have to wait. We found a bench and he began.

"Can God really forgive anything?" The eyes of this twenty-five-year-old student moistened and his voice began to trail off.

"Yes," I said. "Anything." And then I waited. His next words caught me totally off-guard.

"I think I murdered my daughter," he mumbled, staring at the ground between his feet.

As a young pastor I had encountered people with a variety of problems: addictions, broken marriages, bankruptcy, homelessness and sexual misconduct. But murder was new. If there was a time for unconventional wisdom, it was now.

"She was only a few months old," he continued, "and had a terminal disease that was slowly destroying her digestive system. We fed her with a tube as her condition worsened. One day, while I was feeding her . . ." He stopped and fought back tears. "She died. I think she choked on it. I think I killed her. Can God forgive that?"

This may sound strange to you, but along with deep compassion and love for this man, I felt a rush of joy. Because I could offer him something he could not obtain for himself—grace. The unmerited and lavish grace of God that Jesus readily dispenses to thousands of people like this man every day. Grace. Something the ranting courtyard speaker had spoken little of.

This was a broken man who needed to know Jesus was an extreme forgiver, a Savior and friend. I doubted he had done anything to cause his daughter's death. It was a terrible tragedy but not of his doing, and I assured him that God's favor rested on him. Now he needed to forgive himself. We embraced, prayed and talked of this loving, merciful and gracious God. He was relieved. A burden had lifted.

Jesus loves to hear a sincere and heartfelt confession. Not because he has a warped sense of power. Not because he needs to prove his omniscience. *I knew it! Did you think you could hide this from me? Who are you kidding?* Not because he's updating the record books. *That's 348 lies for Donahue this year—wow! I can't wait to see his face on judgment day!* Yet many of us have similar views of God with respect to confession. What will Jesus think of us when we tell him what we've done? Oh, intellectually we know that he knows. But it still feels bad.

Confession is an authentic expression of who we are and what we really do, say and think. That's why it's good for us. Confession releases us from self-deception and self-hatred. God doesn't need to hear our confession—he simply longs to. He knows who we are; it is we who are deceived. To allow Jesus to hear our confession gives him permission to heal us. He already has the right and the power to do so.

I invite you today to approach Jesus as a willing listener. To pray to him. To have a conversation with God—a merciful, loving, grace-giving God. Speaking to God in an authentic prayer of confession is healing and freeing. Brennan Manning describes the freedom that comes when we honestly agree with God about our condition. It's a vulnerable but healing place.

> In our struggle with self-hatred, we obviously do not like what we see. We find it uncomfortable, if not intolerable, to confront our true selves; and so, like runaway slaves, we either flee our own reality or manufacture a false self—mostly admirable, mildly prepossessing, and superficially happy. . . . To pray is to "return to ourselves," where God dwells, and to accept ownership of our sinfulness, poverty and powerlessness. . . . Authentic prayer calls us to rigorous honesty, to come out of hiding, to quit trying to seem impressive, to acknowledge our total depen-

dence on God and the reality of our sinful situation. It is a moment of truth when defenses fall and the masks drop in an instinctive act of humility.

It's in the moment of confession that God's power, grace and truth are most evident. We confess we need him and belong to him, and we ask him to act on our behalf in ways we cannot achieve for ourselves. And Jesus willingly hears and responds. "If we confess our sins, he is faithful and just and will forgive us our sins and purify us from all unrighteousness" (1 John 1:9). I like that last part—as if forgiveness is not enough, God says he will clean up the whole entire mess.

Can God forgive anything?

I'm counting on it.

❧ PERSONAL RESPONSE

What will it take for you to come clean? Jesus is willing to hear your confession and to bring healing to your soul. It's a conversation that will change your outlook on life and your relationship with God.

❧ DIALOGUE WITH GOD

Dear God, I'm afraid—I guess that's my first confession. I know that you already know everything about me. But it's still hard to put my sin into words. I feel ashamed and disconnected from you. Yet I know that this is the only path to freedom, so I am taking a big leap of faith. Grant me the courage to speak truth to myself and to you. And then help me to rest in reality that you are the great forgiver, even when it is hard to forgive myself.

❧ FURTHER BIBLE READING

1 John 1

THE FORGIVER WHO INVITES OUR REPENTANCE

God, have mercy on me, a sinner.

Repentance. Ugh. Isn't confession hard enough? Why add repentance to the mix? Is it not sufficient to simply name what we've done and agree with God that it's wrong? Confession plus repentance . . . that's almost too much, like choking down cough medicine then rinsing our mouth with vinegar. *Repent.* It is not one of the more endearing Bible words. Mothers name their kids Hope or Joy or Grace, but you'll be hard-pressed to find "Repentance Smith" or "William Repentance Owens" on any hospital nursery wristbands. After all, the word conjures up dark images of disheveled men lugging placards up and down the street yelling, "The end is near—repent!" Does the word really deserve such a bad rap? What if there's more to repentance than meets the ear?

Perhaps we have such a shallow understanding of the word because we hold such a trivial view of sin. We've given sin an extreme makeover, smothered it with perfume and dressed it in satin and lace. It's almost a beautiful thing these days, celebrated in art, literature and music. Sin has lost its ugliness, its stench. I remember realizing this for the first time when I heard the words of the1980s hit "Heartbreaker," in which rocker Pat Benatar sings, "You're the right kind of sinner to release my inner fantasies." Hmmm. The right kind of sinner. I guess there are wrong kinds of sinners, too. Axe murderers, child molesters, crack dealers, folks like that. But not fantasy releasers—their brand of sin gets played on the radio.

Don Everts comments that if we ever got a whiff of what sin really smells like, we'd repent—we'd turn and run like a terrified mouse from a stray cat.

The truth is, knowing the reality of sin—the real smell of it—should not depress and deflate us; it should make us mourn our sins and cry out for help. And crying out, in the kingdom of God, is a beautiful thing. . . . The true smell of sin frees us from the smooth, suffocating lies of this age. . . . Talk of repentance and grace and forgiveness rings hollow if sin is just an arbitrary list of fun things we're not supposed to do.

But that's not the prevailing view, even in the church. I sometimes wonder, where have all the sinners gone? We see lots of offenders who make "errors in judgment" and are "sorry if I've hurt anyone." But confessed sinners? No way. It's more popular to admit to facial reconstruction than to say, "I'm a sinner." It's one of the great anomalies of the twenty-first century—no one sins any more. And consequently, no one repents—no one turns and heads the other direction. That's sad, because repentance is one of the most freeing concepts in our world. As Everts says, "Crying out is a beautiful thing."

The New Testament word *repentance* means "a change of mind, a turning away." It goes beyond confession to a change of heart and mind that results in changed behavior. It's more than "I'm sorry." The passionate Jesus-follower Paul instructed a church in Corinth about repentance, reminding them that "godly sorrow [for sin] brings repentance that leads to salvation and leaves no regret, but worldly sorrow brings death" (2 Corinthians 7:10). Godly sorrow grieves the heart, alienates us from God and causes a desire to come home, to return. It loves reconciliation, justice and transformation of character. Worldly sorrow expresses sadness over events but makes no determination to pursue internal, lasting changes. Thus it results in death—spiritual, emotional and even physical. Worldly sorrow produces a change in demeanor; godly sorrow produces a change in destination.

Three days before Christmas one year we moved into a sixteen-year-old home in a wonderful neighborhood. The previous owners had severely neglected the property, making the price affordable and renovations considerable. Strangely, during those few days the frigid December temperatures yielded to an almost springlike fifty degrees. This was great moving weather for December in Chicago.

We couldn't wait to get into the new place. It needed paint, carpeting, minor repairs and some new appliances, but it was home and the view was superb. Our new home rested on a hill next to two small ponds in a neighborhood of about eighty homes. The flat Midwestern terrain allowed us to see for twenty miles out the front windows.

There was only one problem. The outside windows had never been cleaned and were coated with a thick gray substance resembling waxed paper. The layers of dirt clouded out the view of the majestic oak trees and shimmering pond across the street. I took advantage of the unseasonable "heat wave" to wash the windows before another freeze set in. Darkness was looming and I was grateful to get most of them clean.

The next morning the sunlight cascaded through the living room, and we had a clear view of the Canada geese lounging beside the pond. The view was resplendent, capturing our hearts and evoking a sigh from both my wife and me. If it was this beautiful in winter, what would spring and fall be like? I remembered wondering how the former owners could sit here day after day, year after year and allow that grime to slowly blur their vision. Especially with this view! It was beyond reason to me.

Confession says, "Yep, those windows sure are dirty." Repentance says, "Those windows are dirty, it's my fault, and it grieves me. I've ignored the problem. But now I'm going to clean them and start paying attention. When I notice dirt building up again, I'll get to work immediately rather than feign ignorance or pretend the grime will wash itself away."

To identify the dirt of sin and turn from it requires a contrite heart and a change of mind, a new way of thinking that results in changed behavior. Jesus invites this kind of contrition, though he is keenly aware that many of us don't really believe we sin and therefore do not seek God's grace and mercy. So, to make it clear and reveal his own heart about true repentance, he tells us a story, a parable about a tax collector and a Pharisee who came to the temple to pray.

The Pharisee, a pious man of high standing, is self-righteous and proud of his religious accomplishments. He strides brashly into the presence of God and prays about himself. "God, I thank you that I am not like other men—robbers, evildoers, adulterers—or even like this tax collector. I fast twice a week and give a tenth of all I get" (see Luke 18:9-14).

Now there's a humble prayer. *God, thanks that I'm not a loser like these other jokers around here. You must have a hard time even looking at them. I bet you're glad that rule-keeping zealots like me are close by, guys who never miss a service and perform our religious obligations on time, every time. As you know, I work hard at this, above and beyond the call of duty, even fasting more often than the Jewish law requires. We need more guys like me around this place!*

The tax collector, on the other hand, stands "at a distance" from the worship center, smothered in shame and stricken with guilt. These Jewish outcasts who did Rome's bidding at Israel's expense were a despised and detested lot. "Tax collectors," observes Ken Gire, "were the dung on the sandals of the Jewish community." His head sinks downward, his chin finding its home on his heaving chest. Avoiding eye contact with others he glares at the hardened floor of the temple courtyard, a sandstone mirror reflecting the condition of his heart. Fraud and deceit, trademarks of his business, weigh on his conscience like a millstone around his neck. He desperately wants to reconnect with God but secretly wonders if God will ever receive him. There he lingers on the periphery, feeling unworthy to occupy even two square feet of courtyard space let alone enter the temple itself.

Meanwhile the Pharisee has sized up the competition for religious prominence. It is the hour for prayer and the temple grounds are beginning to fill with the faithful and the sinful. Among the worshipers are the riffraff of Jewish society, the bottom rung on the social ladder—robbers, beggars, lepers and adulterers. *Look at this place*, he thinks to himself. *For goodness' sake, how in the world are we going to keep this place holy with all these people desecrating every square inch of it?*

In his eyes he's a ten in the company of zeroes. No competition today. He stands in the light, but his heart is filled with darkness. He longs for attention. He pauses, delivers his oratory heavenward and promptly justifies himself.

Now the tax collector speaks, not so much with his voice as with the pounding of his fists. The thudding sound envelops his despairing but audible cry. He is overwhelmed with remorse. He slumps, delivers his prayer and humbles himself. He longs not for attention but redemption. Jesus says, "He would not even look up to heaven, but beat his breast and said, 'God, have mercy on me, a sinner.'" Though he stands in the shadows, his heart is now filled with light.

Jesus then delivers the kicker. "I tell you that this man, rather than the other, went home justified before God. For everyone who exalts himself will be humbled, and he who humbles himself will be exalted."

Jesus invites a repentant heart, one that brings the seeker home. God's relentless love motivates that change in heart. An awareness of the destructive and ravaging effects of sin, combined with the gracious love of God, works to woo the broken one home where grace and freedom fill the air. Indeed, it is God's kindness that leads us to repentance.

So what stands in the way? Pride, ego, a foggy window pane covered with the dust and grime of a past life? It's time to act—to turn around. And Jesus can help you.

PERSONAL RESPONSE

It's often hard to turn from past habits and patterns, especially certain sinful ones. Reflect for a moment on areas of behavior that are a struggle for you. Are you willing to begin changing some of the patterns and habits that contribute to that behavior? What could you begin to do, in addition to confessing the problem, to turn from behaviors that rob your freedom?

DIALOGUE WITH GOD

Jesus, help me to make a 180-degree turn from the activities and behaviors that bind me. I want to change. Help me to find some safe people who will encourage my progress and pray for my resolve. I need to identify activities that will redirect my passions toward fruitful, God-honoring actions and thoughts. Thanks for giving me your Word, your Spirit and the body of Christ—your people—to guide me in this repentance. And help me persevere.

FURTHER BIBLE READING

Romans 8:1-17

THE FORGIVER WHO CANCELS OUR DEBT

For if you forgive [people] when they sin against you,
your heavenly Father will also forgive you.

Stephen Clark owed more money than anyone could imagine—hundreds of millions of dollars. Not only had he mismanaged his own personal fortune, he had borrowed hundreds of millions from Terrance Owens, a multibillionaire oil tycoon and founder of Owens Global Refining & Exploration. Clark had been hoping to salvage his dying business. Now repayment of the loan was due and he needed more time—lots of it. In reality, he needed a dozen lifetimes to rebuild his business, make it profitable and generate the revenue necessary to write a check for the millions he'd borrowed—not to mention the escalating interest.

As a token gesture of his sincerity to repay the debt, his wife and two sons worked for Owens for free—not exactly the job she wanted after interviewing in the fashion industry. As for his sons, they would rather have stayed in college than work in the office, but there wouldn't be any college anyway now that bankruptcy was imminent. Even with this effort by the family, though, he couldn't put a dent in the amount owed.

"Step into my office, Clark," barked Owens one Friday morning. "Take a seat." The impressive office was lavishly decorated and contained a mahogany conference table, where Owens's corporate attorney and accountant sat looking like they'd just arrived at a funeral.

"Your loan was due last week, and I've waited as long as I can," Owens said. The attorney shuffled some documents while the accountant began some calculations on a laptop computer. "You owe me 274 million."

"Yes sir, I know."

"Plus interest," remarked the accountant, peering over his horn-rimmed glasses.

"So when can I expect payment?" asked Owens.

"I don't know. . . . I . . . I need more time. I think I can really put this together, though. My company is entering into a new venture with a biotechnology firm. They have an experimental hearing device that's a breakthrough in medical technology, and I—"

"Experimental?" huffed Owens. "Come on, Clark. You're talking about five years before it hits the marketplace and another five before you recoup your investment. I won't see a dime for at least ten years! And who's going to finance your deal when you're 274 million dollars in debt?"

Maybe it was the pressure of the moment, but more likely it was the overwhelming reality that Clark could never pay this money back. He was emotionally exhausted, his dark eyes and pale skin reflecting the stress he'd carried for months. He was gaunt, having shed thirty pounds from lack of sleep and loss of appetite. Suddenly Clark burst into tears and slumped onto the table.

For a moment everyone sat stunned. Here was a broken man, a man who had hit bottom so hard the thud could be heard in every office in the building. Owens had never sat at the table with a man who looked like this. He'd cut billion-dollar deals and fired vice presidents at this table. But he had never watched a man's life unravel before his eyes.

Owens uncharacteristically found himself feeling pity toward Clark. Granted, the debt was no small sum, but Owens's Saudi Arabian subsidiary had lost two hundred million dollars in the first year of operation, and another hundred before breaking even. And how about the litigation over drilling rights with the federal government in 1998? Owens was cleared of wrongdoing, but six years of court battles, lost business opportunities and attorneys' fees had cost him another eighty million. Maybe this guy's life was as valuable as a court case—and maybe more so. Oh, what the heck.

"Go home, Clark, and take your family with you," comforted Owens, his hand on the weeping man's shoulder. Clark looked up.

"But sir, it's only 10:30 in the morning and I know there's so much work—"

"Take them home," Owens interrupted. "They're done working here. Let them find jobs elsewhere. Unless they want to stay. In that case, they all need to report to human resources and get put on the payroll. We can discuss specific salaries later."

"Salaries? I'm confused."

"No—you're forgiven. Your debt is canceled. You don't owe me a dime. Go rebuild your business."

The silence from the accountant and the attorney's side of the table was deafening. Had Owens lost it? Was he going nuts? Did he know how much of a write-off this was? There were deals in process in which no one knew the extent of the company's exposure. How could he kiss off almost three hundred million bucks?

"Clark, did you hear me?" asked Owens, looking into the glazed eyes across the table. "Go. It's okay. Simmons here will draw up the legal papers now and I'll have them delivered to you this afternoon, just to make it all official. Now get out of here before I change my mind."

"Mr. Owens, I . . . I don't . . . I can't believe . . . thanks, sir. Oh my. Bless you, sir. I'll never forget this. Never."

Clark and his family practically flew out of the building. They didn't know whether to laugh, cry or scream. At 4 p.m. the documents arrived, notarized with a copy of the loan documents and promissory note with the word "canceled" stamped across the front.

All Clark had to do was sign and return the forms to make it official. This was no dream.

The family celebrated that Friday night at the Oasis, a four-star restaurant across town. They hadn't been able to afford something like this in years. In the middle of dinner a man entered and took a seat across the room, apparently waiting for a business associate to arrive. He didn't see Clark and his family, but Clark noticed him.

Stan Seevers, a former client, had taken shipment on some equipment—twenty-three thousand dollars' worth—and never paid the invoice because he was sued by an angry competitor just days after the purchase. Seevers needed the equipment to keep the business running while he battled the lawsuit, and he had promised to pay immediately thereafter. Unfortunately, he lost and was forced to declare bankruptcy. All company assets were sold at an auction. Seevers got only ten thousand dollars for the equipment and sent it along to Clark, but it was thirteen thousand less than the original price.

"Excuse me a minute, honey," Clark said to his wife as he pushed away from the table. "There's a client over there I want to talk to. I'll be right back."

"Stan? Stan Seevers, right?"

"Yes. And you are . . . ?"

"Stephen Clark, president of Brackford Industries," he said, staring firmly into Seevers's eyes.

Seevers recognized the name and the company and immediately stood. "Uh, nice to meet you, Mr. Clark. Look, about the equipment, I did the best I could when the company folded. Personally, I hope to repay everyone in full some day. But I have to start a new business and it could take a few years. That's why I'm here tonight. I'm meeting a potential partner."

"Potential?" asked Clark incredulously, his voice rising. "I can't pay my employees and feed my family with potential. I want my money and I want it now!" Now he was yelling. "You think thirteen thousand dollars is nothing? Well, it's a lot of cash to me. It better be in my hands Monday morning, or I'll take you to court myself!"

It was an embarrassing moment, and customers at the surrounding tables were watching. So was Seevers's potential business partner, who had just arrived a few minutes earlier and had witnessed the angry remarks by Clark. Now he approached the table.

"Oh, good evening, Mr. Owens," said Seevers. "I'm sorry about all this commotion. I hope you haven't been waiting long."

Clark stood frozen in place. *Owens?*

"Hello, Clark," said Owens. "I must confess I can't believe what I just heard."

"You two know each other?" asked Seevers.

Stephen Clark stood rigid, suspended in time.

"Not as well as I thought," said Owens. "Clark, about our discussion this morning. I'm withdrawing the offer. My attorney will be in touch Monday to begin legal proceedings to collect the funds. Now please excuse us. Oh, one more thing—I never want to see you in my building again. You would ruin a man's life for thirteen thousand dollars? Goodbye, Clark. See you in court."

Some of you will recognize this modern-day parable as similar to Jesus' story in Matthew 18:21-35. A servant cannot repay his master an enormous debt. The master demands that the family be sold into slavery and all family assets liquidated to pay the debt, though even this won't scratch the surface. The servant pleads for mercy. The master is moved to pity and miraculously cancels the debt.

When the servant leaves he encounters a fellow servant who owes him about a hundred days' wages, a significant sum for a laborer by first-century standards. Nonetheless it's a pittance compared to the millions he had owed the master. The man asks for mercy but instead the servant has the debtor thrown into prison. Other servants report what happened to the master, who is outraged. "I canceled all that debt of yours because you begged me to. Shouldn't you have had mercy on your fellow servant just as I had on you?" Listen to Jesus' final words in the parable.

> In anger his master turned him over to the jailers to be tortured, until he should pay back all he owed.
> This is how my heavenly Father will treat each of you unless you forgive your brother from your heart. (Matthew 18:34-35)

The parable is a moving one. We are the servants with a sin debt we can never repay—not in a million years. We cannot work or buy our way out of it. We can only throw ourselves on the mercy of the one to whom the debt is owed. Thankfully, that one is Jesus, the debt canceler. If we do not appeal to Christ, the consequences are chilling. In the parable, Jesus uses the image of a jailer who tortures the debtor until he can repay the debt. Naturally he cannot—especially when he's in jail. Thus the sentence is eternal. Jesus is not portraying God as a torturer. This is a parable. Nonetheless, it reveals the disdain God has for those who refuse to have mercy on others after being forgiven such an enormous debt.

The parable raises a few questions. First, have I acknowledged that I have a debt so great I cannot cover it, no matter what I do? Second, do I believe that Christ's death was sufficient to cancel my debt? And third, am I willing to extend mercy to those who have offended me? When they express grief over what they have done, will I forgive them from the heart, never harboring resentment against them? The choice is mine. The choice is yours.

"Canceled. Paid in full." Some of the most beautiful words we will ever hear.

🎜 PERSONAL RESPONSE

Think for a moment—really think—about the reality that Jesus has paid for and canceled the debt you owe. In light of this reality, what difference will it make in how you relate to God and to people you encounter each day?

🎜 DIALOGUE WITH GOD

Dear God, thanks for wiping the slate—no, several slates—clean. Actually, my sins would probably fill a room full of CD-ROMs. And yet it is amazing that you erased them all, even the ones I can't remember, and especially the ones that have caused so much damage. I know I have to deal with the consequences of my sins, but I feel such relief knowing that I will never have to pay the price for them. Thanks, Jesus. I am amazed at the grace and love you have shown to me.

🎜 FURTHER BIBLE READING

Galatians 2:6—3:4

THE FORGIVER WHO TAKES OUR PUNISHMENT

I, when I am lifted up from the earth,
will draw all [people] to myself.

On January 13, 1982, Air Florida Flight 90 departed from Reagan National Airport in Washington, D.C., for Fort Lauderdale. It was 4 p.m., almost two hours past the scheduled departure time thanks to the winter storm that had been pummeling the East Coast all day. The passengers had boarded at 2:45, after which Captain Lawrence Wheaton commanded that de-icing procedures commence. Snow and ice on the ground were so bad that the plane had to be pulled from the gate by a vehicle with chains on its tires.

Finally at 3:59 the plane was cleared for takeoff. The 737 headed down the runway and ascended over the Potomac River. Suddenly, the nose of the plane rose sharply but the aircraft failed to gain altitude. After a brief stall it fell to the ground, striking the Fourteenth Street bridge during rush hour and smashing into several cars. Five people were killed before the plane landed in the icy waters of the Potomac.

I watched the rescue attempts on television. The darkness of the sky and water was broken only by the white fuselage sinking into the water. News cameras revealed a man eerily balancing atop the aircraft. Somehow he had managed to escape the icy waters and had climbed on top of the fuselage, and he was trying to help others out of the water onto the plane. Icy conditions and the location of the plane prohibited any boat from moving quickly to the rescue. So a helicopter was dispatched with a rope ladder. Because of the chafing wind and icy snow, the chopper could hover only briefly above the entombed craft, just long enough for someone standing on top to grab the ladder and be whisked away.

I watched as the man helped the first passenger grab the rope. A few minutes later the helicopter returned, and he helped a second passenger. It was amazing. Then I began to wonder how he was doing this. Certainly hypothermia was setting in. The blustery winds, increased by the speed of the propeller blades, had to be turning his wet clothing into an icy shroud. But he remained steadfast.

The helicopter returned a third time, presumably to rescue him, but he was gone. Likely he was overcome by the weather and slipped into the river, an icy grave for seventy-four Florida-bound travelers that day. Only five survived the tragedy. At least two of them owe their lives to a courageous unidentified passenger. In a way, he took their place—he gave his life for theirs. Perhaps he expected to survive. Perhaps he thought, *Just one more—I can hold out for just one more.* Or maybe he was one of those rare people who counted the lives of others as greater than his own. We'll never know.

Jesus did not give his life unwillingly. He not only took our place, he took our punishment. And he knew it would happen. Jewish prophets had foretold this seven hundred years earlier.

> We all, like sheep, have gone astray,
> > each of us has turned to his own way;
> and the LORD has laid on him
> > the iniquity of us all. (Isaiah 53:6)

It makes sense to us, or at least we can understand, when someone gives their life for a friend or family member. Or even for a good cause. But it's counterintuitive to sacrifice your life for a meaningless cause or for evil people. Imagine someone willingly forfeiting his life to take the punishment of a Hitler, a Stalin, a Saddam Hussein or a serial killer. Yet Christ gave his life—took the punishment—for evil people like that. And for evil people like us. Paul makes this clear.

> You see, at just the right time, when we were still powerless, Christ died for the ungodly. Very rarely will anyone die for a righteous man, though for a good man someone might possibly dare to die. But God demonstrates his own love for us in this: While we were still sinners, Christ died for us. (Romans 5:6-8)

Last year on Good Friday our church designed a self-guided, interactive service structured around the traditional seven stations of the cross. Simple instructions were provided to help participants stop and reflect on the symbols at each station. Each pointed to some element of Christ's passion. My family—Gail, Ryan and Kinsley—

joined me as we paused at every display, reading the Bible passages provided, praying and pondering. It was deeply personal and moving. Two of the displays especially marked us. One guided us to hold a hammer and spikes similar to those used to nail Jesus to the cross. The other included bread and cups for sharing the sacrament of Communion that Jesus initiated with his disciples the night of his arrest.

I met Christ there in a deeply transforming moment. At first I could only stare at the spikes, my mind conjuring up the vivid images that accompany a crucifixion. Having recently seen Mel Gibson's *The Passion of the Christ,* the scenes were more realistic than they had been previously in my imagination. I heard him panting and pictured his trembling hand, hundreds of onlookers urging me to strike a blow. I put the spikes down after only briefly holding them. And the hammer—my fingerprints were all over it. My hands, pressed downward by the weight of my guilt, made lifting it almost impossible. The realization sunk in of what it really meant for him to "take our punishment." I had to sit down.

The sacrament of Communion also reminded me of the price Jesus paid as he bled and died. When Christians participate in this sacred ceremony, we reconnect with Jesus and his community throughout history. Together we solemnly proclaim that his death brings us life. I felt the guilt falling away and his grace pouring down. Oh I knew I had been forgiven long ago, at age twenty-three when I first experienced the full impact of his amazing grace. But today—on this Good Friday—the sacred act we shared as a family became a declaration of surrender, an act of defiance against pride and ego and self-preservation. I was filled with gratitude and humility, an undeserving rebel basking in the light of a very good God and his extremely forgiving Son. In that moment I returned again to meet Jesus, not just at the foot of the cross, but at the mouth of the empty tomb. I took my part in his death and savored my partnership in his resurrection. We all did. I treasured those moments together—moments of gratitude with my family in the company of Jesus. Moments with some bread, a cup, a hammer and three spikes.

> God, who is rich in mercy, made us alive with Christ even when we were dead in transgressions—it is by grace you have been saved. (Ephesians 2:4-5)

> God made him who had no sin to be sin for us, so that in him we might become the righteousness of God. (2 Corinthians 5:21)

Jesus willingly traded places with us so we could find life. If you're not convinced how incredible that is, just ask the survivors of Flight 90.

☙ PERSONAL RESPONSE

How does it make you feel to know that Jesus stepped in and took your place? What kind of response does that elicit from you?

☙ DIALOGUE WITH GOD

Dear Jesus, the question that comes to mind is, "Why me?" Why would you step in and take the rap for me? You deserve better than that, and I deserve much worse. What kind of God would allow this? What kind of king would permit this? I can only conclude this: an extremely loving and forgiving one. So here I am, standing in awe of you and with nothing but gratitude.

☙ FURTHER BIBLE READING

2 Corinthians 5:11-21

THE FORGIVER
WHO RESTORES OUR RELATIONSHIPS

First go and be reconciled to your brother;
then come and offer your gift.

In the A.D. 120s the Roman emperor Hadrian ordered the construction of a wall in Britain down the valleys of the Tyne and Solway rivers. Its purpose was to separate the growing Celtic tribes from the Romans. Though its seventy-six-mile length was impressive, the wall was not large enough to prevent any formidable attack and could easily be breached by a determined army. Nonetheless, Hadrian's Wall had a psychological effect, stemming the flow of people and communication across cultures. Walls foster a kind of isolationism and self-sufficiency. They always have. Just look at the Great Wall of China and the Berlin Wall.

But we like barriers—they create a sense of safety and security. "Good fences make good neighbors," goes the old saying. But they also drive wedges between people. Years ago we lived in a section of Dallas, Texas, where every backyard was bordered by a six-foot privacy fence. Our personal fortress, backed by an alley that led to our rear-entry garage, fostered isolation, not communication. Most folks hardly saw their neighbors, let alone spoke to them. Personal privacy, not neighborly community, reigned supreme. No one accidentally invaded another's space, and kids and pets were shielded from any spontaneous interactions. We were good neighbors indeed, if "good" means self-contained.

And yet, "Something there is that doesn't love a wall," wrote Robert Frost in his poem "The Mending Wall." That "something" is a longing to be connected to God and to others. To be at peace with them. To live in harmony, like members of an orchestra, playing our individual instruments but producing a beautiful composition, the music of community. Walls, though often serving a necessary and meaningful purpose, often remind us of what separates us, what makes us different and distinct. In the kingdom of God, emotional and spiritual walls are barriers to friendship with God and others.

> You are all sons of God through faith in Christ Jesus, for all of you who were baptized into Christ have clothed yourselves with Christ. There is neither Jew nor Greek, slave nor free, male nor female, for you are all one in Christ Jesus. (Galatians 3:26-28)

One day the Pharisees, a group that prized separation and threw spiritual wall-building parties on weekends, approached Jesus to question him about the Law. One of them asked Jesus to rank the great commandments in order of importance. Instead of falling for this trap, Jesus reduced the hundreds of commands to two, confounding his inquisitors.

> Jesus replied: "'Love the Lord your God with all your heart and with all your soul and with all your mind.' This is the first and greatest commandment. And the second is like it: 'Love your neighbor as yourself.' All the Law and the Prophets hang on these two commandments." (Matthew 22:37-40)

In other words, love God and love people—that's the entire focus of the Mosaic Law and all the prophetic teaching of the Old Testament. Break down the barriers that keep you from God and people. It is very simple, yet so profound. Gilbert Bilezikian, a mentor of mine and founding elder of our church, often emphasizes the cross as a visible symbol of Christ's reconciling power.

The cross, in other words, not only provides for our reconciliation to God in its vertical dimension, but it also makes possible reconciliation among humans with its horizontal embrace. All the designs of God for the creation of the new community are achieved through the cross.

Paul writes in Ephesians 2:13-16 that those of us who were far away from God and one another are "brought near through the blood of Christ," and "through the cross" he reconciled us into one body. God desires oneness with us and wants the same for the people he created, beginning with the Jews and non-Jews of Jesus' day. Paul explains how through Christ, God "has made the two one and has destroyed the barrier, the dividing wall of hostility" and that "his purpose was to create in himself one new man out of the two [Jew and Gentile], thus making peace, and in this one body to reconcile both of them to God through the cross, by which he put to death their hostility."

I returned to my high school's twentieth reunion a few years ago, anticipating that I'd see the effects of aging and maturity (or lack thereof) among the returning alumni. Such reunions are a kind of rite of passage for all who attend. As Gail and I arrived at the hotel, I wondered if Karen would be there. No, she wasn't an ex-girlfriend. Karen was someone I had played a rude trick on at a party, embarrassing her in front of dozens of classmates.

Put simply, I made her the brunt of some crude juvenile humor as part of my ongoing ploy to entertain people and get attention—this was before my life-changing encounter with Jesus. My stunt caused her to run crying from the party as I and my friends roared with laughter. That was the last time I had spoken to her. Now, as I entered this party twenty years later, there sat Karen. Gail, who knew the story, knew what I had to do. And so did I.

After settling in and greeting some of my old buddies, I walked over to her table. "Hi, Karen."

"Hello, Bill. Welcome back."

"I wanted to talk to you about something that happened a long time ago," I said. "I don't know if you remember . . ."

Before I even finished the sentence she remarked, "Oh, I remember." Of course, how could she forget?

"What I did to you was really terrible, and I'm sorry." She nodded and offered a cautious smile as if to say, "I appreciate that."

"This may not mean much to you," I added, "but I have come to know God in a very personal way, and he has done much to change my heart over these years. I have a long way to go, but I wanted you to know that I'm ashamed at my behavior and hope that someday you can forgive me. That's all. I hope you enjoy the reunion."

She was a bit startled but felt my sincerity. "Thanks, Bill. Thanks for saying that."

As I walked away I felt a new freedom. I had been forgiven by Jesus, but now this relationship, broken by foolish sin, had been restored, at least as much as possible. I don't know if she ever fully forgave me, but I was free. I had been reconciled. Though our relationship had never been close, it was important to me—and to Christ—that I do my best to make it right. I felt the joy of heaven and the affirmation of my Jesus, the one who understands the power of forgiveness and the freedom that comes when wrongs are righted and "those who are afar" are reconciled.

Jesus still meets me here often—at the crossbeam of reconciliation. That's because I sin often and drive wedges into my relationship with him and others. His love and grace provoke me to come clean with him and to heal rifts with people I love.

Our God is a relational God, and the destruction of authentic, loving relationships grieves him because it erects a wall of separation. The Bible is clear—sin alienates us from God and from one another. Jesus came to reconcile us with God and restore our connection with each other. The cross was the means of the reconciliation process. His death brings us together—across racial, ethnic, religious and national barriers. And now we can truly be in the company of Jesus, enjoying fellowship with people and friendship with God.

Our choice is to do the work of Christ and be wall-breakers or to destroy that work and become wall-builders.

I'd rather walk across the room and be a wall-breaker.

❧ PERSONAL RESPONSE

Look back at relationships you've had. What makes the good ones thrive and others fail? When there is relational breakdown, what does it take to put it back together? Now reflect on your relationship with God. Are you aware of everything he has done to make a vibrant relationship possible?

❧ DIALOGUE WITH GOD

Thanks, Jesus, for being the glue in my relationships, especially between me and my Father in heaven. And thank you for doing the hard work of reconciliation so that all people who call on your name can enjoy unity, putting away prideful differences and petty resentments. And help me to notice when I re-enlist in the wall-building business. I'd rather tear some down, but I can drift into old habits easily. I need you and some good friends who can keep me on the path. You are so good.

❧ FURTHER BIBLE READING

Ephesians 2

Jesus

THE AUTHENTIC LEADER

He was the emotionally distant son of an alcoholic Midwestern shoe salesman," wrote the reporter at *Newsweek*. He was a "maddeningly contradictory figure," indeed an enigma.

"An eloquent advocate of traditional values, he divorced his first wife and was often estranged from his children. A fierce advocate of balanced budgets, he never proposed one. A dedicated anti-communist, he reached out to the Soviet Union and helped end the cold war. An icon of button-down morality, he led an administration beleaguered by scandals. A man capable of nuanced thinking, he strongly believed in Armageddon."

That man was Ronald Reagan, one of America's foremost presidents. His passing in June of 2004 prompted many to evaluate his character, leadership and legacy. Much admired, even among critics, Reagan was a charming and endearing public figure but a mysterious and elusive man in private. Daughter Patti Davis writes, "There is some solace in knowing that others were also mystified by him; his elusiveness was endearing, but puzzling. He left us all with the same question: who was he?"

Reagan is not the only one of whom the question has been asked. Every great leader or would-be leader faces unceasing scrutiny and analysis, forever being examined at those curious places where public life intersects with a private world. Questions emerge such as, "Is he the real deal? What is she really like? Who is this guy—really?"

Probably no one created more of a public stir than Jesus of Nazareth. His identity, authority and character were challenged at every turn. "Is he the real deal? And if so, what do we do with him?" Some family members thought he was crazy (Mark 3:21); religious leaders questioned his authority to forgive sins (Luke 5:21); people in his hometown challenged his identity (Mark 6:3); even his closest followers were often befuddled by his actions and asked, "What kind of man is this? Even the winds and the waves obey him!"(Matthew 8:27).

Authentic leaders often cause a commotion by the very fact that they are true to their convictions, thoughts and emotions. There is no posing, no posturing, no image management to ensure a consistent, predictable persona. Jesus was authentic—and he was anything but predictable. His righteous indignation could be aroused one moment and his loving compassion the next. This was not the mark of a schizophrenic; rather it was the trademark of a person who could express emotions and yet never lose control of them.

Jesus' authenticity also demanded that he lead his disciples as a servant, because that's what he was: "being in very nature God, / [he] did not consider equality with God something to be grasped, / but made himself nothing, / taking the very nature of a servant, / being made in human likeness" (Philippians 2:6-7).

God is a servant. That's his nature. He loves by serving and he leads by serving. He's the real deal.

In order to lead we need to come to the end of our own power. "We all have fears, flaws, frustrations or fantasies that get in the way of being God's people," writes Marva Dawn. "Instead of pretending to 'have it all together,' can we learn to admit our weaknesses so that the power of God can be manifested in, in spite of and through us?" Dawn struggles with kidney dysfunction, a crippled leg, blindness in one eye and deafness in one ear. She has learned to be a channel for the power of Christ as it flows through her broken body. She teaches and leads in weakness, as does her Savior.

We need more leaders like Jesus—authentic servants who are not afraid to serve and are not afraid to lead. Jesus was such a leader.

THE LEADER WHO RELEASES OUR STRENGTHS

Come, follow me, . . . and I will make you fishers of men.

"He has your best interests at heart." Ever heard that one? When the Branch Davidian compound in Waco, Texas, was razed by fire in 1993, everyone inside thought that cult leader David Koresh had their best interests at heart. When over nine hundred people committed suicide in 1978 in Jonestown, Guyana, everyone who drank the Kool-Aid believed Jim Jones was doing what was best for them. More recently, stargazing followers of cult leader Marshall Applewhite donned their black shirts and Nikes, and then took their lives as the Hale-Bopp comet blazed across the night sky in 1997. Followers were certain that he was guiding them to a celestial nirvana.

Messiahs have enticed followers in every age to forsake everything and follow them. Was Jesus any different? Did he really have us in mind? Or, like many self-professed saviors before him and since, did he care only about himself? Did he want his followers to flourish, or did he want to exploit them for personal gain and notoriety, commanding a level of devotion and sacrifice that, in the end, simply fed his ego? As a leader, would he be more interested in waving his own banner or would he find joy in seeing others' colors flying high? A closer look at his words is revealing.

> I tell you the truth, anyone who has faith in me will do what I have been doing. He will do even greater things than these, because I am going to the Father. (John 14:12)

No insecurity, no turf protection, no jealousy on the part of Jesus. When he was only one or two years into his public ministry, Jesus gave his disciples great authority and power for the work of ministry, releasing them to use their strengths—underwritten by his power.

Few leaders are secure enough to allow us to soar as high as God has gifted us. They often have a hidden agenda that will not allow them to authentically be "for us." Behind each forced smile and affable slap on the back lies a hidden suspicion that we may become more popular, more effective or more influential than they are. An oversized ego fueled by insecurity and fear prevents such leaders from enthusiastically supporting those under their leadership.

But Jesus was truly "for" his disciples. Though he wanted them to rely on his abundant strength and power, he took great pains to empower and release them.

> When Jesus had called the Twelve together, he gave them power and authority to drive out all demons and to cure diseases, and he sent them out to preach the kingdom of God and to heal the sick. (Luke 9:1-2)

Jesus also knew that every strength has a weakness associated with it. Peter's impulsive courage on the Sea of Galilee ("Lord, tell me to come to you") was rivaled by his disbelief that Jesus must suffer and die ("Never, Lord! This shall never happen to you!"). Because of this ambiguity in people—to affirm our trust and deny it later—Christ allows us to venture out on our own like exploratory two-year-olds who think they're alone climbing that ladder, even though Dad is standing right there.

Our Jesus is wise. He releases us—he does not abandon us. We remain in his company. "I'll be with you as you do this," he says, "day after day after day, right up to the end of the age" (Matthew 28:20 *The Message*). He's taking a huge risk on us, but he knows that in his presence our strengths can be utilized and our weaknesses redeemed for his glory.

Do you have the courage to be set free—free to serve as Jesus empowers you? It's quite a thrill. And don't worry; you don't even have to leave the planet!

❧ PERSONAL RESPONSE

You have strengths. Have you surrendered them to God for his use? Invite him today.

❧ DIALOGUE WITH GOD

Jesus, release my strengths for your glory and redeem my weaknesses. Help me to see that I am useful not because you need me but because you desire to use me and take joy in my success. That's an amazing reality. I have come to see that my strengths are your gifts to me and that my weaknesses are my gifts to you. Help me use both of them well, for your purposes, and in your name.

❧ FURTHER BIBLE READING

1 Corinthians 12

THE LEADER WHO ALIGNS OUR VISION

Why do you look at the speck of sawdust in your brother's eye
and pay no attention to the plank in your own eye?

Like many people in their forties, I have found that my arms are getting too short for reading. I often prided myself on my ability to read
signs at great distances, long before others could even see the sign.
"Eyes like an eagle," my mom would say. And while I still have much
of that ability, reading words twenty inches from my face has become
increasingly difficult, requiring reading glasses. An eye exam revealed
that my left eye is weaker than my right. They are not aligned, at least
with respect to each eye's ability to perceive light. Normal age-related
degeneration combined with this alignment problem makes things a
bit blurry these days. Like many of you, I now have prescription eye-
wear to correct and align my vision.

Mine is a common and easily treated condition. Other problems
are more serious, the result of injury, heredity, nerve damage or simple neglect. For some, blindness is a condition from which they will
never recover. One thing is clear—vision impairment requires help;
it cannot be solved on our own.

Vision impairment is also one of the great spiritual diseases plaguing
our culture. Either we do not see the truth at all, or our vision of spiritual truth is out of alignment with God's as revealed in the Bible. It takes
a leader like Jesus to help us see clearly and align our vision with God's.

Some, however, cannot see the truth. Some choose not to; others dis-
pute its existence. In his monthly column "My Current Opinion," Guy
Spiro, a proponent of the New Age movement, writes the following:

There are many paths in the search for God, perhaps as many
paths as seekers. I have always been amazed at the audacity of

anyone saying that they know the Truth and that someone, or anyone, else is wrong. Like little boys arguing over whose dad could beat up the other's, it is just as silly when proponents of religions argue over whose is right. . . . Think for a moment. Is it possible that God, if for a minute we even think of him having a gender or personality, would care if we come to him through one faith or another? Would he not recognize worship if it were directed through a tree? My own current opinion is very well summed up in the quote, "I looked for God everywhere and found only myself. I looked for myself and found God." Let us all find God in whatever form or system works for us and leave others to do the same.

Spiro has a strong conviction that people should not have strong convictions. At least, that's his current opinion, which could change at any moment to the opposite opinion, held with just as much conviction. Clear as mud, right? Sounds like the person who is absolutely certain there are no absolutes. This is vision impairment—what the Bible labels spiritual blindness—and it was the most difficult disease for Jesus to heal. To be clear, he had the power to heal it; it's just that in many cases healing was contingent on cooperation of the patient. Doctors can prescribe medication and recommend lifestyle changes—which patients choose to accept or reject. The response of followers and seekers alike to Jesus often depended on their ability to see what he was plainly doing or saying. As the great ophthalmologist, he spent a great deal of time addressing vision problems, opening the eyes of many and rebuking others who willfully shut theirs to the light.

For some, improved vision required a minor corrective procedure; other situations demanded extensive surgery. In almost all cases, peo-

ple had no idea that their vision was out of focus. However, after an
eye exam from Jesus, patients became acutely aware of how spiritually blurry they were. If you look at the eye chart in Jesus' office, it
reads something like this:

> The light shines in the darkness, but the darkness cannot un-
> derstand it.

> Blessed are the pure in heart—they will see God.

> Remove the plank in your eye before the speck in your
> brother's eye.

> The blind will see, but those who can see will be blind.

Jesus courageously confronted the spiritual astigmatism of his day,
a condition that caused people to view God's kingdom in distorted
and backward ways. Jesus had to intervene with corrective surgery to
help them—and us—see the real king and understand the realities of
the true kingdom. His kingdom was not designed for those who were
enamored with political power, built oppressive hierarchies, hoarded
wealth, dispensed punishment at a whim or promoted spiritual elit-
ism. Instead, the kingdom was available to everyone, especially the
poor and persecuted. It was filled with mercy and grace, governed by
compassionate lovers and ruled by justice.

So how's your vision? Blurry? Out of alignment? It may require corrective lenses or an outpatient procedure. Is it difficult for you to see
the truth that's just inches from your face? It's probably time for an extensive exam. Reflect on your view of Jesus and his ways of doing life,
his values and his teachings. Then read the Gospel accounts in the
New Testament, even if you've read them before. Ask yourself, Do I
see people how Jesus does? Do I view the world as he does? Do I understand power and truth and community and wisdom as he does?

Then pray. Ask him to diagnose and prescribe.

And be courageous enough to do what the doctor says—even if it's a radical surgical procedure.

There's a whole new world of truth, hope and joy out there. I wish you could see it.

PERSONAL RESPONSE

How long has it been since you let someone examine your spiritual eyesight? I wonder what it would be like for you to understand your degree of blindness, what's causing it and how to remedy it?

DIALOGUE WITH GOD

Jesus, I want to see. I admit that I am blind. At best my vision is out of focus and blurry. I know it's risky to ask, but the prospect of seeing you and the world in a fresh new way is worth the risk. So change me. Open my eyes to see you clearly.

FURTHER BIBLE READING

John 9

THE LEADER WHO DEMANDS OUR DEVOTION

*If anyone would come after me, he must deny himself
and take up his cross daily and follow me.*

When Ernest Shackleton set out to traverse Antarctica, cutting across the continent from Weddell Sea to Ross Sea, he took twenty-seven men with him. Little did they know that it would be five hundred

days before they set foot on land again. The infamous voyage, chron-
icled masterfully in Caroline Alexander's *The Endurance: Shackleton's
Legendary Antarctic Expedition,* describes a journey of courage, perseverance and loyalty. No one had ever crossed the entire continent of
Antarctica. Shackleton had set out for the South Pole in 1908 and
surpassed Robert F. Scott's 1903 attempt, but severe illness forced
him to turn back just ninety-seven miles short of the goal. This time
he was determined. It would be a grueling trip and Shackleton
wanted only the best men.

The Endurance set sail for Antarctica from South Georgia Island in
December 1914. Soon the ship was trapped in pack ice that surrounded the continent, imprisoning the vessel and carrying it eight
hundred circuitous miles. The men were unable to free the ship, and
eventually it was crushed and sank. With only a few lifeboats and
limited rations, the men sailed one hundred miles in seven days to
Elephant Island. Then they attempted the impossible. Shackleton
took five men and set sail for the whaling station on South Georgia
Island, their only hope for rescue. Leaving an officer behind with the
others, the six sailed a twenty-three-foot lifeboat over eight hundred
miles in stormy, icy seas. Seventeen days later they reached the
island. It was a sailing accomplishment for the record books. That
none perished on the journey is a virtual miracle.

But once again Shackleton and his men faced overwhelming odds.
They had landed on the uninhabited side of the island. To make contact with the civilization they had to climb steep cliffs, navigate icy
peaks and traverse vast glaciers on foot. Remarkably, they survived
this ordeal as well, reaching the whaling station at Stromness. Even
then, it took four attempts over the next three months in horrible
conditions before they successfully returned by ship to Elephant
Island where the rest of the crew remained. They were astonished

and overjoyed to find everyone alive. They had all survived twenty months in a freezing hell.

The sailors were unanimous. Despite moments of doubt and thoughts of mutiny, the crew's loyalty to Sir Ernest Shackleton remained firm. He had led them through trials but had never subjected them to conditions he would not bear himself. They loved and respected him. He demanded their best and always gave them his. Anything less would have cost lives.

Great leaders, authentic leaders, demand loyalty. For Jesus, this meant 100-percent devotion to him and his cause. When his followers vacillated in this area, he reminded them of the high cost of following him and the great expectations associated with the venture.

We are also called to this unwavering and persevering devotion. Only ruthless trust in Jesus and his leadership will guide us to our ultimate destination. But the pathway of discipleship is no easy road. It's covered with thorns and lined with crosses. Some of the thorns may find their way under our skin, and we can be certain one of the crosses has our name on it. Loyalty to Jesus means devotion even unto death. It's not pretty, but it is rewarding. Paul said, "I have been crucified with Christ and I no longer live, but Christ lives in me. The life I live in the body, I live by faith in the Son of God, who loved me and gave himself for me" (Galatians 2:20).

Shackleton's team had given up everything short of their lives. Their destination was unknown, the journey strenuous, the odds overwhelming and the prospect of failure high. And indeed they failed. But some failure has its own reward. "In memories we were rich," Shackleton wrote. "We had 'suffered, starved, and triumphed, groveled down yet grasped at glory, grown bigger in the bigness of the whole.' We had reached the naked soul of man."

Paul Cody observes of Shackleton's journey, "Exploration brings surprise, hardship and unexpected rewards. Just a few steps past the darkest, unplanned moments lies the deepest fullest grace. That is the point of going out there."

Unlike Shackleton, Jesus knew his destination, understood the road he would have to travel and looked forward to its rewards. His "failure" would mean our success; his loss our gain. We share not only in the fellowship of his sufferings but also in the glory of his resurrection. And unlike Shackleton, to rescue us cost him his life.

In love he has given us his all. In return he demands our loyalty. Our loyalty for his love—that's more than fair. I think we get the better part of the deal, don't you?

❧ PERSONAL RESPONSE

Loyalty is a difficult thing. Much rests on the object of our trust. In this case that object is Jesus. Is he worthy of your loyalty? If so, are you willing to meet his demands? They are not light. He wants all of you. Picking up the cross is an act of dying to self. Are you ready for this? You may be more ready than you imagine. There's a whole company of Jesus-followers doing the same. Will you join us?

❧ DIALOGUE WITH GOD

Dear God, this is one of those hard teachings. To be honest, I'd like to cut it out of the Bible. But I cannot. This road you call me to walk is hard, but I know Jesus has already been here because there are bloodstains on the path. It was much harder for him than it will ever be for me—and he had to do it alone. Thanks for helping me by providing the strength of Jesus and your Spirit, and for surrounding me with others on the same journey. I'm afraid but trusting. Take me; I am yours.

✎ FURTHER BIBLE READING

Luke 9:18-27

THE LEADER WHO REDEEMS OUR FAILURES

You will all fall away.

If at first you don't succeed, skydiving is not the sport for you. Or so the saying goes. Despite the fact that few failures turn out to be fatal, nearly all feel final—at least for the moment. In November 1974 my high school football team was well into another losing season. We had won four games in three years, and it was likely that our record would be one-nine again this year. We were so bad that other schools scheduled us for their homecoming and parents' days.

It was the ninth game of the season and I was chosen to be defensive captain of the week. The reason we had a new captain every week was that no one wanted the honor for the entire season. "And now let's introduce the captains of the worst team in the league for the third consecutive year . . ." No thanks. One week was bad enough.

As defensive captain my job was to instill motivation and provide leadership to the defense, to help eleven young men function as one, to stop the opposing offense right in its tracks. "No one scores on us! No one completes a pass play against us! This is our day!" I also had to learn the hand signals the coaches used from the sidelines. These signals had to be complex enough that the other team couldn't decipher them yet clear enough for the captain to understand so he could relay the information to the huddle. Sometimes it was hard to tell whether our coach was sending signals or swatting at bees. In any case, signals were important because they described where to line up on the field, special actions to be taken by certain players, when to blitz the quarterback and so on. Our tactics were designed to confuse the other team's offense and then overpower them with our amazing strength. A big challenge for the smallest team in the conference.

For that ninth game we faced the number one team in the league, with an all-state quarterback and a pass receiver who was also a track star holding the state record in the quarter-mile sprint. Not a problem. We had the right signals, the right plays, home field advantage and a great defensive captain—me. Put that all together and what do you get?

You get slaughtered, that's what. It was the worst loss in the school's history. There I stood, staring at the scoreboard as it ticked off the final seconds . . . 3, 2, 1, 0. When the final whistle blew it read "Eagles 53, Panthers 0." Yes, our defense had courageously held our opponents to a mere fifty-three points while our well-rested offensive team dominated the bench.

That loss stuck with me a long time. It was hard to shake the shame. I know Churchill said, "Success is never final; failure is never fatal. It's courage that counts." He's right. But he never played football for the Panthers.

No one enjoys losing. Whether in school, sports, business, the arts, you name it—people want to succeed. And failure is often seen as fatal, at least through the eyes of the one failing.

One of the most popular failure stories of the Bible is Peter's denial of Jesus just before his crucifixion. Unwilling to be identified with the "criminal" Jesus and fearing a similar fate, Peter disowns Christ three times, just as Jesus had predicted (Luke 22:31-34). As a teenager hearing the story I often wondered, "How could you, Peter? How could you turn your back on your best friend?"

Then one day I did the same thing to my friend John. Several other ninth graders and I had cajoled John into placing a firecracker in a milk carton in the lunchroom on the last day of class. After it exploded and covered several students with a bubbling, milky foam, a teacher who had observed the fiasco escorted the six of us, still laughing, to see the principal, Mr. H. When asked, "Who is responsible for this?" John confessed, "I did it."

Mr. H. continued, "And who urged him on? Did anyone coax John into performing this foolish deed?"

Howard answered yes, and the principal promptly called his mother on the phone. "Do you know what your son Howard was involved in today?"

Suddenly this was not so funny. Most of us feared our parents more than the principal. I was next and I was a tough guy, so I did what any tough schoolkid would do.

I lied. And the others followed suit. "Not me. It was John's idea," we said.

I'll never forget the expression on Howard's face. It said, "You weasely little wimps!" John's eyes spoke volumes as well. "Thanks for hanging me out to dry, guys. Some friends you are."

The attitudes and reactions we experience in school don't stay behind when we graduate. No diploma erases them. Fear of failure, or of being associated with failure, still evokes expressions of denying, blaming or fleeing. Peter's exasperated words to Jesus in Mark 14:29-31 are instructive: "Even if all fall away, I will not. . . . Even if I have to die with you, I will never disown you."

It's easy to write off these words, saying, "There goes Peter again, impulsive and rash." But the end of verse 31 catches me off-guard, leaving me naked and ashamed like Adam and Eve after tasting the forbidden fruit. Mark writes, "And all the others said the same." Of course they did. We would have as well.

But their failure was not final. Before telling Peter he would fall away, Jesus said to him, "Simon, Simon, Satan has asked to sift you as wheat. But I have prayed for you, Simon, that your faith may not fail. And when you have turned back, strengthen your brothers" (Luke 22:31-32).

Jesus understands failure. But he understands restoration even better. He is a true leader and so, to encourage his followers, he redeems our failures, refusing to let us languish in them. I can hear the echo in his words to Peter: "And when you have turned back . . . And when you have turned back . . ." There is hope and redemption for every act of failure, and for failures like you and me. When we return to Jesus, carrying the broken pieces of our lives in our hands, he turns failure into ministry. *Strengthen your brothers. Give away the grace that I gave you in failure. Freely you have received—freely give.*

Don't be dismayed by what you see on the scoreboard of your life. Jesus has a way of turning a fifty-three-point loss into a kingdom victory. Trust me, I know from experience.

PERSONAL RESPONSE

Have you accepted the fact that failure is not final, or are you wallowing in self-pity and shame? Can you come to grips with the transforming truth that Jesus can redeem failure?

DIALOGUE WITH GOD

Dear God, can Jesus really take my broken life and use it? I mean, have you looked closely at this mess I've made? I want to believe that I can and will turn back, and that you will dispense grace to me and channel ministry to others.

✤ FURTHER BIBLE READING

John 21

THE LEADER WHO REWARDS OUR OBEDIENCE

If you love me, you will obey what I command.

We all want our kids to obey us. Granted, sometimes it's because we have control issues. But most often it's because we love them and understand their obedience as a return expression of love. We have their best interests at heart and want them to succeed, avoid danger and learn discipline. But sometimes they make other choices. They want to be independent and buck authority. My own kids are pretty good, but they push the edge as they strive to carve out a life of their own. Maturity means learning the difference between independence and disobedience. It's a challenge for adults and children alike. Reinhold Niebuhr, in *The Nature and Destiny of Man*, says, "Sin is the unwillingness of man to acknowledge his creatureliness and dependence upon God and his effort to make his own life independent and secure."

Yes, "independence" can simply be a euphemism for disobedience.

I love watching classic Christmas movies with my family over the holiday season, especially with a cup of hot cider by a warm fire. Some are deep and meaningful, some silly, but most have a message worth celebrating or pondering. One of my favorites (and admittedly one of the sillier ones) is the animated classic *Rudolph the Red-Nosed Reindeer*, narrated by the plump, Santa-like Burl Ives. My kids love it and I love it. You know the plot. Rudolph, an object of ridicule for his prominent schnoz, and Herbie, a misfit elf who'd rather become a dentist than make toys, are shunned by their peers and feel obliged to move away. They meet, realize their mutual misfortune, and agree to pursue a new life.

> "I don't need anybody," says Herbie. "I'm . . . I'm . . . independent."
>
> "Me too. I'm . . . whatever you said," echoes Rudolph. "In-de-pen-dent."
>
> "Hey," says Herbie enthusiastically, "what do you say we both be independent together!"

I love that last line—independent *together!* Though there is a certain pleasure in shirking all authority and obligation and heading out for adventure, there is also the need for others. No one really wants to be alone. Yet the drive for independence is so strong, it can even push us beyond adventure to rebellion, disobedience and irresponsibility.

Adam and Eve disobeyed so they could be "just like God" and have it their way, to create a life on their terms. We know the result: relational discord and breakdown between one another and with God. When people under authority disobey, they do not simply reap the consequences of their actions, they undermine their relationship with the one in authority.

Obedience is first and foremost a relational term. In the Old and New Testaments the word is always tied to God and his relationship with his people. And it is ultimately motivated by love. Every parent knows this. To obey is to honor the relationship and demonstrate love. For this, God grants a reward.

So what is this reward? What do we get when we obey Jesus' commands? Wealth, security, possessions, God's cell phone number? Listen to Jesus:

> Whoever has my commands and obeys them, he is the one who

loves me. He who loves me will be loved by my Father, and I too will love him and show myself to him. . . . If anyone loves me, he will obey my teaching. My Father will love him, and we will come to him and make our home with him. (John 14:21-23)

What do we get in exchange for obedience? We get God. He takes up residence in our spiritual home. Jesus and the Father (and the Holy Spirit as well) move in—not for the weekend, not just for Christmas and Easter, but forever. The Creator of the universe, the Almighty God, the Holy One says, "We will come and live with you—we'll do life together. I like being in the company of those who love and obey me."

Our culture has an entitlement mindset. We expect to be served, provided for, protected, fed, employed and cared for. We believe these things are owed us and we demand that they be provided when and where we need them. But this mentality fosters not only a gratitude gap, it causes us to look at God as a distributor of goods and resources that we deserve as his children. We are likely to think less about how we can love and obey him and more about what we can get from him.

When Jesus walked the earth, the wind obeyed him. The waves obeyed him. Evil spirits obeyed him. People, however, did not always obey him. And that hasn't changed much in the last two thousand years.

We tend to miss the whole point. When we obey Jesus, we don't "earn" God; he's our reward. That's why obedience is a relational concept. The English word *obey* means "to hear toward" or "to submit to the control of," which is why we can obey our passions, our instincts, our conscience, our teachers and so on. When we obey, we place ourselves under the authority of God and we listen to his voice. As a result we feel his love.

We love to obey because we love God. Obedience yields rewards that are practical (wisdom, success, protection from evil) and personal (deeper fellowship with God).

That seems more than reasonable. God want his kids to obey just like we do—for our own sake.

PERSONAL RESPONSE

Obedience is not a popular term today. It implies submission and humility. What is your attitude toward obedience? Do you easily and readily desire to do what God has asked?

DIALOGUE WITH GOD

Dear God, I want to obey. But I admit that sometimes I want to obey you on my terms. I want a special reward—an answer to a prayer, help finding a job, money or a vacation. I can easily drift into the "what have you done for me lately?" mindset, forgetting that I owe you everything. Help me to remember that obedience is an act of love, not simply a chore or an obligation. I do love you. Help me to show it more often.

FURTHER BIBLE READING

Psalm 119

6

Jesus

THE COMPASSIONATE
HEALER

As I write this I am settling into seat 28H on a Lufthansa flight from Frankfurt, Germany, to Capetown, South Africa, by way of Johannesburg. It's 9:45 p.m. and I have thirteen hours of commercial air travel ahead of me. Thirteen hours of inhaling the airborne germs of 280 passengers. Thirteen hours of sitting in economy class (another term for "cattle car"). Thirteen hours next to an Italian man from Venice who has little interest in sharing the two-and-a-half inches of armrest space between us. I do have one advantage over most passengers—my seat faces the bulkhead, providing three feet of extra leg room.

After the passengers finish boarding and the door closes, every seat on the plane is occupied except 28K, the window seat in our row. Blissfully the Italian chap leaps into it so there is a one-seat gap between us. "Now we have some elbow room!" he says, grinning, and leans his pillow-supported head against the glass, eager for several hours of nocturnal unconsciousness.

Most people on crowded flights secretly pray for a one-seat gap. There's extra room to maneuver and an extra tray table for drinks so you can use yours for working. The gap also helps you forget that you're wedged into economy class like size-eleven feet in size-ten shoes—especially when the flight attendant reads those special instructions for your fellow passengers in the front of the plane: "For those of you seated in business and first class, feel free to use your portable DVD players and Internet connections throughout the flight. We will begin serving prime rib and lobster tail shortly, so please return your oversized vibrating-massage lounge chairs and footrests to the upright position. This will also help us navigate the aisles when we move through with the French pastry and liquor carts. For those in economy class, we'll be coming by when we feel like it to serve you a microwaved muffin and soft drink—limit one per customer."

For the first hour of flight my Italian friend and I sleep, grateful for the extra room the bulkhead affords. Right now I couldn't be happier. I can stretch out my legs and no one in front will recline their chair into my lap for nine hours. I awake to the sounds of food service moving down the aisle and seize the moment to visit the lavatory before eating a light meal, and before taking a mild sleeping pill that guarantees me four to five hours of needed rest. In nine hours we'll be in Jo'burg, then a short hop to Capetown.

As I return to my seat, eager for my hibernation, I think I've made a mistake. A woman is sitting in my place, her husband and eleven-month-old son occupying the middle seat. I notice my now agitated Italian friend, and realize this is indeed my row. "Excuse me," I say politely, "but I think you're in my seat. I have 28H." The woman's head turns briefly, and then she returns to the task at hand, designing a makeshift bed on the floor for her son with some pillows and blankets. The father is holding the child and settling comfortably into 28J, previously the only vacant seat on the plane. No more one-seat gap.

"She's not staying, but he and the infant are," remarks the flight attendant, observing my confusion. "They have two small children and I decided that, since 28J is open and has the bulkhead, they might like the extra room. So I'm moving them here."

Just sixty seconds ago I had the prime seating. Now an airline-backed coup has taken place and the extra gap has vanished, along with my optimistic expectations. An eleven-month-old boy is lying on the floor where my long legs would have gratefully extended, and he's banging his plastic cup saying, "Ga ga ga!" Nine hours of this lies ahead.

I'm headed for ten days of teaching, after which my family will join me for some vacation and serving among the poor. Our itinerary includes trips to an AIDS home, two visits to black churches in challenging areas, an afternoon on Robben Island where Nelson Mandela was imprisoned and a visit to the Apartheid Museum. We want to combine sightseeing in Capetown and Johannesburg with ministry. Some larger churches there are having up to seven AIDS-related funerals a week.

As I ponder the trip in my head, the irony begins to set in. I hear the clear voice of Jesus as if he were in 29H behind me. "Bill, you're willing to travel halfway around the world to extend grace and hope in South Africa, but you're blind to the opportunity to show compassion to this family right next to you. What are you thinking?"

For the first time in ten minutes, I actually see this family. I find myself smiling at the baby and pondering his future. I begin talking with the tired and overwhelmed father, and I remember how Jesus responded.

> When he saw the crowds, he had compassion on them, because
> they were harassed and helpless. (Matthew 9:36)

The man next to me is black and his wife is "colored," a term South
Africans coined during apartheid days when the government separated blacks, Indians, Asians and coloreds (people who had one
black parent and one white parent) from whites. Compassion for the
man wells up inside. There he is, two small children and a wife to
care for, on an all-night ten-hour flight, with a racial background that
has likely led to few friendships and probably even fewer social en-
gagements. He sits on a plane filled mostly with whites, people who
probably have never felt the racial hatred that lingers in a barbed remark or scornful glance. I am finally able to lend a helping hand, say
a few kind words and offer some comfort to this man and his son as
they slowly drift off to sleep.

When Jesus, the compassionate healer, enters our life, he fills us
with his own compassion. That's how he distributes his love and
grace—through people. I need a compassionate healer, and I need to
become one for the sake of others. Come, Jesus. Show us the way.

THE HEALER WHO CRIES OUR TEARS

Jesus wept.

Kim and I met in the fourth grade. He was Korean American, the eldest son of an American G.I. who had married a Korean woman after
the war there. As with most military kids he moved often, and I met
him in the middle of the school year when he showed up in class.

"This is Kim," the teacher said, and immediately I was drawn to
him. His smile was broad, his eyes bright and, I soon discovered,

his mind sharp. We walked home that day together and almost every day afterward. It was the beginning of a great friendship. We laughed at each other's jokes and helped each other with schoolwork. Actually, I helped Kim throw a football and he helped me with homework—sounded like a deal to me. We were soon best friends.

We entered junior high two-and-a-half years later and still walked home, even though others took the bus. There was something magical and lighthearted about our daily jaunt across the highway, along the woods and through the cornfield next to our neighborhood.

One day that routine changed forever. During a tumbling exercise in gym class, Kim injured his neck. Though there was no apparent nerve or muscle damage, the pain persisted and then intensified. A couple of months later doctors discovered that Kim had spinal cancer. Either the accident had contributed to it or exacerbated the problem. In any case, surgery and radiation ensued, leaving Kim confined to a bed set up in the living room of his home.

For the next two-and-a-half years he lay in that bed. I visited him at least weekly, often more. We'd sit for hours and talk. And we'd laugh. Kim's parents said I was the only one who could bring laughter to his heart and a smile to his face amid his suffering and pain. Then, for a few months he improved dramatically and our hopes were boosted. Kim was able to use a walker and even ventured outside in a wheelchair the October of our eighth grade year. We had a brief catch with the football—well, I did some throwing and he was able to do some catching. The air was cool and Kim was able to smile and dream of days when full mobility would return.

But those dreams were short-lived. Kim's condition deteriorated dramatically that winter and worsened in the spring.

On the first day of school in ninth grade a classmate asked, "So how is Kim doing?" I had to look him in the eyes and say, "Kim died last night."

The memory of that day is surreal. There I sat, surrounded by thirty students who were catching up on the events of summer and lamenting the start of another school year. I sat behind my desk, facing a teacher whose words I did not hear in a room I cannot recall on a day I'll never forget. In my mind, I was somewhere else that day. I was with Kim.

I didn't cry at school. Tears came in the night, and again at the funeral a few days later. The reality of death and loss and separation cut deep. Watching Kim's father and mother grieve at the coffin of their firstborn was more than I could bear. I can still hear the wailing. It all seemed so very wrong.

This was not how life was supposed to be. You were supposed to be best friends, grow up, graduate, get jobs, get married, go to church together, see ballgames with your kids, live to be ninety-five and then die. Death was for old people, something that happened to grandma and grandpa.

Death I had come to accept. But now I encountered dying, and I found it to be twisted and cruel, producing nothing but agony and grief.

Perhaps this is what Jesus felt at the tomb of Lazarus. The Bible, in John 11:35, simply says, "Jesus wept." It's the most human, most intimate description of Jesus in the Scripture. But it's not one we often see in the portraits people paint of the Savior. Yes, we are enamored with his teaching, bask in his love and find ourselves speechless at his miracles. But a weeping God? What do we make of that? I'd rather have the idol-crushing, sea-parting, wall-tumbling God. Doesn't a weeping God belong in a twelve-step group or clinic? Who wants to worship a vulnerable, weeping God?

You do. And I do. Here's why.

What is more elemental to the human soul than the shedding of tears? It separates us from all other living things. Animals don't sob uncontrollably at the loss of a fellow member of the species or mourn their dead for days. To weep is to express the soul of humanity. It's how we communicate love and grieve loss. We weep at the sight of a vacant seat at the table. We mourn the cool, unrumpled side of the bed once occupied by one who gave us unbridled warmth and love. Every song, every smell, every piece of clothing, every familiar pathway reminds us of the loss, reminds us of the tender hand we once grasped or the lips we once tasted. Lovers, family, friends—to lose them is more than we can bear. Tears flow freely at the mention of a name or a glance at a photograph.

Jesus mourned the loss of Lazarus, a close friend, even though he knew he would soon raise him from the dead. What made Jesus cry? Why didn't he simply say, "Hey everyone—the time for crying is over. I'm here. Remember the fish and the loaves, the blind man and the storm on the sea? I'll turn those frowns into smiles in thirty seconds!"

I think the Son of Man wept because he had no alternative. It was the full expression of his humanity. If Jesus couldn't weep at the death of a close friend, surrounded by grieving family and neighbors, then he may have been God but he was no human. The assertion that "the Word became flesh" would have been a cruel hoax.

But instead Jesus was "deeply moved" and wept. Even before he arrived at the tomb, as he encountered Mary, Lazarus's sister, and other mourners on the way, he wept. Jesus shared their tears because he shared their humanity.

Perhaps his tears were shed for us and not simply for Lazarus. Perhaps he cried for the harsh reality of death and dying, the ultimate consequence of sin. Perhaps he remembered the garden he created, the beauty and wonder of a race designed for intimacy with God and community with one another, and he grieved for the loss of innocence. Perhaps the sight of red-eyed, sleep-deprived mourners at a gravesite evoked sorrow and compassion for what they had endured the last few days. Perhaps, like me, he wept because it was all so wrong and could have been so right.

Jerusalem did not want a weeping God. When Jesus approached the city on his journey to the cross, he foresaw her destruction as the prophets had warned. Once again he was deeply moved at the effects of sin and the carnage it leaves in its wake. If only people had believed in him.

> As he approached Jerusalem and saw the city, he wept over it and said, "If you, even you, had only known on this day what would bring you peace—but now it is hidden from your eyes. The days will come upon you when your enemies will build an embankment against you and encircle you and hem you in on every side. They will dash you to the ground, you and the children within your walls. They will not leave one stone on another, because you did not recognize the time of God's coming to you." (Luke 19:41-44)

Most people are not looking for a weeping Messiah. A conquering king, a spiritual superhero, yes. A God who cries? No thanks. But this is the only God who can heal, who can redeem, who can wipe every tear from our eyes. This Jesus, this man of sorrows, this one acquainted and familiar with grief—this is the God who comes down to us. This one who laughs and sings and prays and loves and breathes and, yes, even dies, to bring us back to the Father.

But this Jesus is no tomb-dweller. Neither his death nor his sorrow was final; tears no longer trickle down his face. Resurrections tend to have that effect. One day, when the resurrection work is complete, there will be no more weeping for us either—not for Kim, not for Lazarus, not at all. There will be no tears to cry.

> Now the dwelling of God is with men, and he will live with them. They will be his people, and God himself will be with them and be their God. *He will wipe every tear from their eyes.* There will be no more death or mourning or crying or pain, for the old order of things has passed away. (Revelation 21:3-4, italics mine)

Until then, I will serve the God who wept. And I will give him my tears.

✤ PERSONAL RESPONSE

What keeps you from letting Jesus embrace your tears? Embarrassment? Shame? Fear? Pride? Can you follow a weeping God who brings you strength in your weakness?

✤ DIALOGUE WITH GOD

Dear Jesus, thanks for knowing. For knowing not only the beautiful and amazing aspects of life in the world you created, but also the ugly, broken, painful moments in a world we corrupted. Thanks for not leaving us behind. Thanks for understanding tears and for wiping them away. In my sorrow please be my strength. In my grief, point me to hope. And thanks for a future without tears.

✤ FURTHER BIBLE READING

John 11

THE HEALER WHO BINDS OUR WOUNDS

He had compassion on them and healed their sick.

I just received an e-mail that displays the amazing power of God to bring healing to the wounded. This month, members of our church welcomed a beautiful baby boy into the world. He was a bit jaundiced but otherwise healthy. One week later, he fell asleep while feeding and never awoke. His parents tried to revive him and called 911. But he "slipped away and went home to Jesus," the mother writes. Here is part of the note she shared with us:

> We had called our small group from the quiet room in the ER and let them know where we were and what had happened. From that moment the events were in motion to make Willow a very small church.
>
> Once our small group was aware of the event they called other leaders. Before we left the hospital that evening, our group and church leaders were with us and did not leave our side. We stayed with our parents and they took over the practical things like picking up pizza and other necessities from the grocery store. Friends came over and prayed with us, and by 9 p.m. the staff had called to arrange a memorial service. They made phone calls and helped us put the service together in just two days.
>
> We were expecting maybe sixty people, but when I turned around the chapel was packed. We were amazed. We are still amazed. We get at least one phone call or e-mail a day, just seeing how we are. People are bringing meals to us, and they are planning to help us with yard work this weekend.
>
> Thank you for being such an amazing church. I don't know

what we would do if we did not have the small group structure or our friends from the Newly Married Connection and the Young Families Connection. I am sure that the next several months we will be going through the ups and downs of grief, but it is a great comfort to know we are not going through it alone, that we have friends and family at Willow Creek to walk with us through our valley.

No church is perfect. But when the body is working right and the people of God act as a community in the company of Jesus, his healing, comforting power and healing grace are richly displayed. These people were the body of Christ acting in the power of the Spirit to help a family begin healing from a deep, lasting wound. They fulfilled the words of Peter, who said, "Each one should use whatever gift he has received to serve others, faithfully administering God's grace in its various forms" (1 Peter 4:10). Healing grace administered through the body of Christ is a beautiful thing to behold.

Sometimes God heals directly—immediately, theologians would say. But much of the time his wound-binding ministry is mediated through others. Others stand as go-betweens, connecting hurting people to God's healing power. Jesus desired his church to function this way, so he exhorted the disciples in Matthew 9:35-38 to pray that shepherds would rise up to bring healing and comfort to wandering, wounded sheep. These shepherds prompt others (like small group members and families) to be Christ to one another in times of tragedy, danger and despair. This is the nature of God and the nature of the community that bears his image. "He heals the brokenhearted / and binds up their wounds," writes the psalmist (Psalm 147:3). Indeed, he is "that great Shepherd of the sheep" (Hebrews 13:20).

Jesus did not live in a wound-free zone. During his public ministry he faced accusations, threats and incessant questioning by people who sought his demise. His career ended in humiliation, torture and death. He understands our wounds because they are his. By his wounds we are healed. We receive his healing and his righteousness. He gets our sins and our wounds. Nice trade.

When I find myself crying out to God to bandage my wounds, he often uses people to do so. The great physician enters my life and dispenses the healing balm of his grace and comfort at no charge to me. No need for insurance, either; he's already paid the bill. His medicine comes not in bottles but in bodies—in hands and feet, in hugs and smiles, in words and prayers.

> Praise be to the God and Father of our Lord Jesus Christ, the Father of compassion and the God of all comfort, who comforts us in all our troubles, so that we can comfort those in any trouble with the comfort we ourselves have received from God. (2 Corinthians 1:3-4)

Let us come together in his name and help one another walk through the valley.

PERSONAL RESPONSE

Our wounds run deep. The emotional and spiritual ones seem most devastating—and most embarrassing. We can keep them to ourselves or reach out for healing to the body of Christ. Are you willing to allow Jesus to work through others on your behalf?

DIALOGUE WITH GOD

Dear God, thanks for people. For their love and their prayers, their hands and their hearts, their healing words and warm embraces. Some of my wounds run deep and the healing will take time. But you give me the gift of community and family and friends. Jesus is there among them, loving me in them and healing me through them. Oh, there are scars, but they are the reminders of a wound healed, a grace given, a life mended. Thanks for being the great physician—and for your amazing medical team. Continue to heal me, I pray.

🎵 FURTHER BIBLE READING

2 Corinthians 1

THE HEALER WHO CARRIES OUR BURDENS

Come to me, all you who are weary and burdened,
and I will give you rest.

It was a moment of terror and desperation, an epic struggle between humility and pride. I can almost feel it today. There I lay, alone on the second story of our home in Pennsylvania, more than 150 pounds of weights across my chest. How did I get there? I ignored a common law in any risky endeavor—use the buddy system. I chose not to.

I was in the middle of a brief workout, lying on the bench somewhere around the tenth repetition. A little voice taunted me, "C'mon, you wimp, don't stop now! Pump out one more!" Instead of putting the weights on the rack above my head, I took the dare and lowered the bar one more time to my chest as I stared at the ceiling, my back pressing firmly against the bench. The bar touched my chest and I pushed upward with all the strength my sixteen-year-old body could muster, trying to extend my arms once more. There was just one problem. The bar rose only three inches above my ribs and came down with a thud.

So I was flat on my back with 150 pounds across my chest and no strength to lift the weight onto the storage rack above me. No one was home. I thought, *I'll reach over and slide a few weights off of one end, and then a few off the other. A few plates will drop to the floor, but no real damage will be done and no one will know any better.*

But there was another problem. I had put a safety lock on each end of the bar to keep the plates from sliding during my workout. So I lay breathing heavily under the crushing weight. I was getting weaker and the weights felt heavier every second. If I tilted to one side, the bar would slide across my chest, slamming the plates against my ribs. If it rolled toward my neck it would choke me. What I chose to do next really mattered.

Let's leave me under the bar for a moment and look at what Jesus does with the things that weigh us down in life. (Don't worry, I'll be all right.)

Jesus encountered many kinds of people in his day—slaves and soldiers, criminals and kings, Pharisees and fishermen, tax collectors and businesswomen, lepers, blind men, rich young rulers and traitors. Each person was unique, yet each had the same problem. They were all trapped under a weight they could not budge with no one to help lift it. For some the weight was a physical impairment, for others a mental illness and for a few it was demonic possession. Many nursed emotional wounds: rejection, shame, bitterness and envy, to name a few. But all shared a common ailment: sin. They were separated from the God who loved and created them for his purposes. It was a burden too heavy to bear. Yet religious leaders of the day felt it necessary to add to the burden. "They tie up heavy loads and put them on men's shoulders, but they themselves are not willing to lift a finger to move them" (Matthew 23:4). Legalism, shame and contempt were heaped on sinners whose knees buckled under the guilt they already felt.

In stark contrast to the Pharisees and teachers of the law, Jesus offered to help carry the load.

> Take my yoke upon you and learn from me, for I am gentle and humble in heart, and you will find rest for your souls. For my yoke is easy and my burden is light. (Matthew 11:29-30)

"Easy" and "light"—two words you won't find in the Pharisees' training handbook.

"Yoke" referred to a rabbi's interpretation of Torah, the Law. The Pharisees put a heavy yoke on people—robes, regulations and rituals. Jesus' teaching was a light yoke, one that gave freedom and help for people carrying the weight of guilt and shame. Jesus' statement was a play on words as people pictured the wooden beam an animal carried as a metaphor for the Pharisees' teaching.

Why do we insist, then, on carrying our own burdens—the weight of our sin or the stubbornness of our pride? Perhaps we've become comfortable doing so. Like the prisoner who continues to haul around the steel ball that was once chained to his ankle, we find comfort in the familiarity of our burden. We carry the weight willingly, like a badge of honor, a statement that we can make it on our own. Forget the fact that we can't run because of the weight. Never mind that our arms are numb and our shoulders ache. That's just life. Besides, everyone carries one—they're quite fashionable. Some are painted, some glossy, some brass, a few even made of gold. The heavier the better.

Yet how free we can be without the ball and chain! Yes, we'll have to figure out what to do with our hands—and to rediscover running. We'll look odd as we float past weighed-down groups sharing stories about their colorful shackles and comparing custom-made spheres. "Yes, this is heavy," they say, "but someone's got to carry it."

And that's the whole point. That someone is Jesus, who takes the heaviest of burdens—our sin—on himself. For everything else he gives us his yoke, his power and grace to go on. He provides loving commands, which "are not burdensome" (1 John 5:3), and a loving community that can "carry each other's burdens" while each one responsibly shoulders his own load (Galatians 6:2-5).

It's time to exchange our yoke for Jesus'. He invites us to use the buddy system, with himself and his followers as partners.

Take my advice. Don't lift a heavy load alone. You'll get yourself in quite a mess.

Which brings me back to those weights I was holding on my chest. I was too proud to call for help, even though a neighbor would doubtless have responded to my yelling through the screened windows. Thankfully, I managed to gradually roll the bar down my ribcage, across my stomach to my hips, until I could sit up. Despite the pain and bruises this caused, relief finally came as I reached the locks and removed the weights.

Praise be to the Lord, to God our Savior,
> who daily bears our burdens. (Psalm 68:19)

PERSONAL RESPONSE

What would it be like to be free from the burden you carry? Are you willing to release it to Jesus? Are you willing to let others help?

DIALOGUE WITH GOD

Dear Jesus, there are many times I want you to carry my burden while I do nothing. Other times I cling to my junk—my anger, pride, disillusionment or self-pity—because it's all I know. Forgive me. Give me your yoke. I trust it will fit comfortably and do the job mine cannot.

✺ FURTHER BIBLE READING

Isaiah 40:28-31

The Healer Who Covers Our Shame

Your sins are forgiven.

I confess I wish I had his freedom, his nerve. He didn't seem the least bit inhibited. He just pulled his shirt up over his head, slid his pants and undershorts to his ankles, stretched out his arms, tilted his head to the heavens, closed his eyes and basked in the warm sun. Jordan was a friend of my wife's and mine. We'd known him almost a year and talked with him almost every day. He ate with us, went to church with us and even played some golf with me. Never in all our conversations had I envisioned him doing something like this. He was not mentally challenged or disturbed as far as I knew.

But for some reason, in broad daylight with half the neighbors watching, he just did it. Right there in the yard, high noon on a Saturday morning in the spring. We all laughed, but I admit I envied him. We all did. We wanted his joy, his freedom, his spontaneity. Like Adam and Eve in the garden, he stood there glorying in God's creation. To our surprise, he was stark naked and loving every minute of it.

Jordan was not ashamed.

Jordan didn't care what others thought.

Jordan was three years old.

We saw Jordan from our kitchen window, and we saw his mother across the backyard through her kitchen window. She was busily working at the sink and hadn't spotted her son in all his bare-tushed glory. So we called her on the phone.

"Hi Becky, this is Bill and Gail."

"Hi guys, what's up?" she asked, still looking down at the sink, phone wedged between her shoulder and her ear.

"How's Jordan?"

"He's fine. Right now he's out back here—*ahhhhh!*"

Watching her run out the back door with a towel was almost as fun as watching Jordan. Becky covered him up and explained the virtues of wearing clothes in a fallen world while we had a few good laughs.

I never forgot the image. I couldn't help but wonder how it all began long ago in the garden. A couple so free, so alive, so connected with God and his creation that it was very good, and they were naked and unashamed.

That was then. This is now.

The bliss of Genesis 2 soon gave way to the destruction of Genesis 3. Humanity exchanged freedom and intimacy for the chance to be just like God, and the result of this disobedience was shame. Suddenly nakedness no longer meant freedom but exposure. Humans' sinful condition became plain for all to see. Adam and Eve needed someone to cover them, and God did, with animal skins. Blood was shed so that their shame could be covered. It was a hint of things to come.

The word *shame* implies hiding, "a covering up." We feel shame because we have disgraced and dishonored a holy God. Sometimes we try to hide our shame by covering it ourselves. But our busyness does not cover it, and neither does alcohol, sex, medication, work, shopping, religious activity, sports or charity work. Only Jesus can cover shame, dressing us in his righteousness. "Blessed is he / whose transgressions are forgiven, / whose sins are covered" (Psalm 32:1).

Someone else needs to do the covering. That's why people whose backs were bent by shame came out of hiding and sought Jesus. They uncovered themselves so that he could cloak them in his righteousness. The religious elite hid their shame behind their traditions and customs; the wealthy hid behind their riches. But those who knew their shame and came out of hiding discovered freedom. A woman caught in adultery, a Pharisee sneaking out to see Jesus at night, a prostitute washing his feet with her tears, a lame man lying by a pool hoping for a touch of mercy. All of these probably felt shame—all of them sought the covering of Jesus.

How about you? Are you willing to bring your shame to Jesus? Only then will you be free.

It feels incredible to live free of shame, to be truly alive, to enjoy each moment basking in the grace and wonder of God. It really does.

Just ask Jordan.

✤ PERSONAL RESPONSE

What would it take for you to be free? To no longer see your shame when you look in the mirror? Are you willing to come out in the open, in the presence of Jesus, who can cover your shame?

✤ DIALOGUE WITH GOD

You can have it, God. I don't want it. My shame and sin are exposed by the light of your truth, and I blush. It's a public disgrace. I'm naked and embarrassed; I need a spiritual makeover and you're the only one who can provide it. Cover me. Cover my ugliness with your transforming grace and holiness. Everything I've tried is window dressing, a superficial attempt to mask the nastier parts of me. But you make me shine. Just thinking of the forgiveness you offer is a breath of fresh air. Set me free, and I will bask in the light of your love forever. With a heart of gratitude I pray this.

✤ FURTHER BIBLE READING

Luke 7:36-50

THE HEALER WHO RESTORES OUR COMMUNITY

That they may be one as we are one . . .

As part of a training program I entered I was required to participate in a small group experience for ninety minutes each week. The group was led by a woman, and the members included nine women and one man—me. This was not a church-based or religious group of any kind. As a matter of fact, no more than one or two of us had had any regular church involvement. The goal of the group was to be real, to be open and to "work on our issues."

Each week I struggled to participate. I'm not sure why, except perhaps that it was a twelve-foot-by-twelve-foot room with no windows, ten women and me. The leader simply said each week, "So, what will we talk about today?" Silence usually ensued. Sometimes someone would complain about a husband, a failed marriage, struggles at work or problems in graduate school. But we never seemed to get beyond that. I became disconnected and began to enter my own private world, remaining aloof and distant.

On the fourth week of the ten-week program a woman looked straight at me. "I don't like your posture here," she said. Everyone stared at me.

"Okay," I quipped, shifting in my chair and crossing my legs. "How's this?"

My sarcasm landed flat. Ten sets of eyes glared at me. "I'm just kidding," I said, trying to hide my discomfort.

"Really," said another woman. "I've noticed it too. You don't seem to be with us. You don't seem to care."

In reality I didn't. And that was the problem. No—*I* was the problem. Jean Vanier writes,

> Community life brings a painful revelation of our limitations, weaknesses and darkness; the unexpected discovery of the monsters within us is hard to accept. The immediate reaction is to try to destroy the monsters, or to hide them away again, pretending that they don't exist. Or else we try to flee from community life and relationships with others, or to assume that the monsters are theirs, not ours. . . . Community life is the place where the ego is called to die so that people become one body and give much life.

Here in this group of women, a group with whom I thought I had little in common, Jesus met me. He was calling my ego to die. He was showing me my pride and insecurity. He wanted me to change. And he wanted me to love these people as he would. It was a wake-up call I needed.

Here's the irony. I was the small group pastor at a growing church. My job was to help people find and experience authentic community and to seek the power of Christ to change their lives. But in this setting I was violating almost every value I stood for. Why? Why was it so hard in this place? As I began to look inside my heart I found some answers. I wanted community on my terms, led by my agenda and supportive of my personal goals. I was also afraid to be known by people I might never see ever again. So I shut them out and hid myself from them.

I didn't like what I saw in myself that day. But there, in the company of Jesus (who I discovered was also sitting in that room), I was confronted with the real me. I wanted to live a protected life, hiding parts of myself from others so they would see only what I wanted them to see. In this way I remained in control. What I didn't realize was that by hiding myself from others I was blocking my growth, hindering my relationship with God and others. I was also blocking the formation of true community in that group. My "posture" of indifference affected group cohesion. And Jesus wanted me to engage, to become part of the restoration—not fragmentation—process.

That moment of realization was a turning point for me. Today I'm learning to fully engage in my groups—family, small groups, teams. I realize that in these relationships Jesus is present and at work. He is restoring communities that have been fractured by our pride, insecurity, anger, selfishness or simple indifference. He calls me to contribute to the process of community building. As a result I find healing, personally and in the community itself.

Perhaps that's why Jesus prayed so fervently for oneness among those who desire to follow his ways. So essential was this theme that it was the primary focus of his prayer life on the eve of his crucifixion. "I pray . . . that all of them may be one, Father, just as you are in me and I am in you" (John 17:20-21). Commenting on this prayer, Gilbert Bilezikian writes,

> The very last thought of a person usually expresses the passion of his or her life. A loving wife on her deathbed will think of her husband, the workaholic of his accounts, the addict of one last shot, the miser of his gold, and the wounded soldier dying on a distant battlefield of home. For Jesus, the central passion of his life was the new community. He had come into the world to reconcile humans with God. He had taught reconciliation and lived it, and now he was dying for it. Understandably, therefore, during the last moments of quietness with his followers, he

prayed for the community of reconciliation. He knew there could be no such community unless it had oneness; thus, he prayed for their oneness.

Division and relational breakdown run rampant today. We are a deeply divided nation, politically, religiously, economically and socially. The issues of war, same-sex marriage, religious expression, abortion, environmental concerns and economic policy are divisive, to be avoided at all costs at social gatherings and business meetings. If you want to drive a wedge into the middle of a group of people, take a strong stand on one of these issues.

Despite our personal convictions and unique personalities, Christ longs for his community to act with one heart and one mind. People in the company of Jesus put aside petty differences and express sacrificial love, serve the poor, reach out to the hurting, comfort the sick, stand for truth and promote justice. When others observe the Jesus community in action, they begin to see a new reality, a people acting as one to extend the love of God to a fragmented world.

This oneness, however, requires a letting go of self. Paul writes, "Do nothing out of selfish ambition or vain conceit, but in humility consider others better than yourselves. Each of you should look not only to your own interests, but also to the interests of others" (Philippians 2:3-4). When we embrace this attitude, pride and self-promotion yield to humility and servanthood, and onlookers see a refreshing lifestyle worth exploring.

Jesus may not place you in a small room with ten women (or ten men) to confront your self-sufficiency and draw you into community life—though that might be the best thing that could happen to you. If that's what it takes for you to change your posture, then so be it.

I know I changed mine—without crossing my legs.

❧ PERSONAL RESPONSE

What will it take to help restore the oneness in your community? In your relationships? What can you do with others to pursue the oneness Jesus prayed for?

❧ DIALOGUE WITH GOD

Dear Lord, I know you prayed fervently for oneness. It's just what we need in this world. But first we need it in our own lives—at work, in school, at church, wherever we meet people. Forgive us for losing sight of the vision, for settling for second best, for following our own agenda instead of the ways of Jesus. I admit I'm often part of the problem; help me become part of the solution. Help me set aside my tendency toward isolation and pettiness that wears me and others down. We all long for a real taste of community life—for oneness in spirit, in mind, in heart. Help me to lead the way. Give me a vision for your future, not mine. And help me pursue it in the company of Jesus and others he places in my life.

❧ FURTHER BIBLE READING

John 17

Jesus
OUR RELENTLESS LOVER

M‌y daughter's preschool class used to sing this rhyme:

Love goes around in a circle,
One by one, two by two and four by four.
Love goes around in a circle,
And comes back knocking at your front door.

I used to think it was a cute song—a bit corny. The kind of song especially designed for children. After all, children need the assurance that love is always available, always seeking them out, always coming full circle. A few times at parents' day my wife and I would visit the school and inevitably be asked to sing along—with hand motions.

It was silly.

It was corny.

It was definitely for children.

And it was very much like the way of Jesus.

In Jesus, the love of God comes knocking. Sometimes when we least expect it, always when we least deserve it. It is the full-circle love of a relentless lover.

> A lover who includes the unlikely
> > ordinary fisherman,
> > > powerful centurions,
> > > > impoverished widows.

> A lover who accepts the unwanted
> > unclean lepers,
> > > outcast prostitutes,
> > > > disruptive children.

> A lover who befriends the undeserving
> > corrupt tax collectors,
> > > rebellious prodigals,
> > > > prideful Pharisees.

Love comes rapping at the door . . . again and again and again.

Here I am! I stand at the door and knock. (Revelation 3:20)

When we accept and receive that love, when we open the door to the love of Christ, our capacity to love others increases, as does our motivation. In fact, our love for one another is evidence that the love of God resides in us. The Jesus-lover John, who had firsthand experience of the love of Jesus, calls us to practice loving God's way.

> Dear friends, let us love one another, for love comes from God. . . . This is love: not that we loved God, but that he loved us and sent his Son as an atoning sacrifice for our sins. Dear friends, since God so loved us, we also ought to love one another. No

one has ever seen God; but if we love one another, God lives in us and his love is made complete in us. (1 John 4:7, 10-12)

This is a mystery to me. God's amazing love is somehow distributed through me to others, and yet somehow I ultimately benefit. Dallas Willard, commenting on this remarkable expression of love, writes, "Here, then, is the full account of the movements of love in our lives: We are loved by God who is love, and in turn we love him, and others through him, who in turn love us through him." Full-circle love. Relentless love.

That's the love of God. A love that keeps returning to the unlikely, the unwanted and the undeserving. It comes our way again.

And again.

And again. Full circle.

THE LOVER WHO INVITES OUR INTIMACY

I will come in and eat with him, and he with me.

I boarded the commuter flight from Dayton, Ohio, to Chicago one Saturday afternoon after a speaking engagement at a local church. It was a routine flight, the cabin half-full with about fifteen people on board. We landed safely in Chicago and taxied to the gate. The flight had been uneventful, but all that changed at the gate. We stopped about twenty feet short of the parking zone and the plane was suddenly surrounded by security personnel. Looking out the window I saw four black, unmarked vehicles unload men wearing earpieces and sunglasses. They approached the ramp and escorted a young man with a baseball cap off the plane, down the jetway steps and into a Ford Excursion with tinted glass.

Obviously we were dying with curiosity. "Probably some senator's kid," remarked one passenger. "Maybe they were transporting a prisoner somewhere," another offered. The flight attendant soon set us straight.

"It was Prince William."

Prince William? The future king of England? The son of Charles and Diana? I was traveling with royalty and didn't have a clue!

I was disappointed—but the women on the plane were devastated. They'd missed their chance to chat with the handsome young prince. "So what are you doing these days to keep busy, Willy?" they would have asked. But none of us knew he was traveling among us. He had slipped onto the plane dressed like a typical college student, wearing a ball cap and sunglasses. He was one of the last people to board, along with a security agent or two, I'm sure. Who would have expected a prince to ride a commuter jet with a group of average Americans from Dayton (of all places) to Chicago? No one. Not even those of us who sat a few rows behind him recognized the heir to the throne.

The prince had wanted privacy, not intimacy—at least not with us. I can't say I blame him, especially based on the reaction of the single women on the plane once they discovered that one of the richest, best-looking, most eligible bachelors in the world had been flying with them, trapped at thirty thousand feet for an entire hour with no place to run.

Liesel Pritzker is ten times richer than Paris Hilton, heiress to the Hilton Hotel fortune. At age nine she starred in the movie *A Little Princess* and later acted alongside Harrison Ford in *Air Force One*. Today, at only twenty-one years of age, she is worth more than $1 billion and has about $160 million cash in the bank. She attends an Ivy League university and will never have a financial worry the rest of her life. So, with all her millions, what did she do in high school in her spare time?

According to a reporter at the *Chicago Tribune,* she drove an unassuming Volkswagen Golf and worked at a deli.

She chopped onions, waited on customers and rang up orders. "She was great," says store owner Mitch Cobey. "She did anything I asked. . . . Of the students who've worked for me, she was one of the top two." Asked if it surprised him that a girl with $160 million wanted a job, Cobey is, for a second, uncharacteristically silent. "I wasn't aware that she had $160 million," he says.

She was friendly—not snobby—to other students at the elite New Trier High School in upscale Winnetka, a north suburb of Chicago. A classmate recalls that "there were girls at the school who would look you up and down and just keep walking." Apparently this was not so with the down-to-earth Liesel (who is named after the eldest von Trapp daughter in *The Sound of Music*). "She always would smile at you in the halls and say hi," says a former fellow student.

We are often surprised when the high and mighty or the rich and famous "dip down" and walk among us commoners. Hollywood stars and business moguls cannot afford it. Doing so might taint their images or tarnish their relational networks. After all, it's reaching up the ladder, not dipping down, that gets your picture on the society page. Princes and kings likewise are busy with the demands of royalty—international guests to meet, polo matches to attend, public appearances to schedule, wardrobes to manage, officials to greet and family members to please. Royalty can ill afford to invest much time hanging around folks near the bottom of the social ladder. Well, with one exception.

The King of kings, Jesus, not only dipped down, he stayed down. He was not forced to work us into his calendar; he desired to spend time with regular people, choosing twelve of them to sit at the royal

table with him. Among us he ate meals and took walks and attended
worship services and went sailing.

He came to reveal himself, not to hide his true nature. He was God
with us, Immanuel. He walked among us without security guards or
escorts, lived in no royal palace, managed no trust funds and held no
memberships in private clubs. He was not too preoccupied with running a universe to hang out with us. He was "my friend, the king."
And he wanted no casual relationship but rather a close and personal
friendship. He still does, even today.

> Whoever has my commands and obeys them, he is the one who
> loves me. He who loves me will be loved by my Father, and I too
> will love him and show myself to him. . . . If anyone loves me, he
> will obey my teaching. My Father will love him, and *we will come
> to him and make our home with him.* (John 14:21-23, italics mine)

> I have made you [the Father] known to them, and will continue to
> make you known in order that the love you have for me may be in
> them and that *I myself may be in them.* (John 17:26, italics mine)

The King of the universe wants intimacy with us. He wants to lead
us, love us and enjoy us—forever. All he asks in return is simple obedience to his loving commands as an expression of our love for him.
As I see it, that's a small price to pay for dining with the King.

Unless we'd rather settle for traveling with royalty and not even
knowing it.

Not me. I'd rather have dinner with my friend, the King. Want to
join me? There are plenty of invitations to go around.

✨ PERSONAL RESPONSE

Intimacy with God might sound odd or make you feel uncomfortable. Why is this so? Is it hard to view him as a close friend? Or is it just the idea of intimacy in general? Why is getting close to God a wonderful yet fearful experience—often at the same time?

✵ DIALOGUE WITH GOD

God, I admit that sometimes I'm scared to death by your closeness, even though I long for it. I want to know you, but I fear that when you get to know me, you may not like what you see. Yes, God, I know that you already know. There are no secrets with you. I guess I'm still trying to figure this intimacy thing out. I need it but am terrified at what it might be like.

Help me remember that long before I even thought of loving you, you already loved me and were planning to send Jesus as an expression of that love. Please understand I want to know Jesus and his love fully. But it still feels awkward, like a blind date or wondering what your college roommate will be like, or the morning after the wedding when you think, Do I really know this person? It's a mysterious adventure. Help me embrace the mystery—and learn to return your loving embrace.

✵ FURTHER BIBLE READING

John 14:15-27

THE LOVER WHO DESIRES OUR FAITHFULNESS

As the Father has loved me, so have I loved you.
Now remain in my love.

"Our love for God is sacred," says Scot McKnight. "Love is sacred because genuine love is total in its commitment . . . and survives only when it is held in honor."

No one stands at the marriage altar, makes a vow and hopes his or her partner will be unfaithful. It is inherent in the marriage covenant to remain faithful "till death do us part," and it is central to our love relationship with God. His third commandment is clear: "You shall not make for yourself an idol . . . for I, the LORD your God, am a jealous God" (Exodus 20:4-5). Later, at the second giving of the Ten Commandments, after the first stone tablets have been destroyed, God intensifies his passion for his lover. "Do not worship any other god, for the LORD, whose name is Jealous, is a jealous God" (Exodus 34:14). God does not simply express jealousy—his name is Jealous. God competes with no other lover. To reject his love is to commit spiritual adultery.

Today's rising generation is a step ahead of the game—or a step behind, depending on how you look at it. Instead of risking the heartbreak of unfaithfulness, they just don't make a commitment in the first place. If there are no promises, there are no promises to break. For the last few years this practice of noncommittal love, primarily found among college students, has been given a name: a "hookup." A hookup is a one-time sexual encounter—anything from kissing to intercourse—between acquaintances who may not even talk afterward or ever see each other again. Psychology professor Elizabeth Paul surveyed 555 undergraduates and found that 78 percent had hooked up, especially after using alcohol. The average student participated in just under eleven hookups during four years of college. A "good hookup" was defined by one woman as an experience in which "no one finds out about it or talks about it later." Now that's commitment.

If you have a pulse you are aware that this behavior is not limited to college students. As I write this chapter the hottest show for primetime viewing is *Desperate Housewives,* a serial drama in which married women seduce their neighbors' husbands, gardeners and stray delivery men who wander within thirty feet of the doorstep. The hype and enthusiasm among women for the show is even more troubling than the content.

Infidelity is on the rise among women, so much so that *Newsweek* devoted a cover story to the trend in July 2004. Over the last ten years the number of married women who've had sex outside marriage has risen from 10 percent to 15 percent, edging closer to the 22 percent of married men who do the same. "He tells me my skin is soft and that my hair smells good. I know it sounds stupid, but that stuff matters. It makes me feel sexy again," remarks a thirty-nine-year-old woman who married at age fifteen and has been seeing a boyfriend for the last five years. Women want to be loved and cherished, and often their marriages provide neither. So they explore readily available (and easily hidden) relational opportunities at work, on the Internet and on business trips. But the hunger begins at home when marriages fail to live up to expectations. "Couples begin to live parallel lives instead of intersecting ones, and that's when the loneliness and resentment set in."

No wonder God uses the marriage-adultery-divorce metaphor to describe our love relationship with him. There is such a thing as spiritual promiscuity. And it grieves God more than we know.

Jesus desires our faithfulness. He wants us to hold our love for him in honor. He is the bridegroom and the church is his bride. The marriage bed of heaven is sacred, requiring a pure and faithful union with Christ. It literally is a marriage made in heaven.

Why do we fall so easily for other lovers? Why do we turn from God and give the best of our devotion to work, sports, hobbies and money, or to less honorable pursuits like pornography, gambling or drugs? Perhaps we live parallel lives with God instead of intersecting ones. Yes, God and I are related and we live under the same roof. We see each other briefly at meals (for grace) and bedtime (for a brief prayer or devotional reading) but our paths rarely cross throughout the day. God does his thing and we do ours.

It's a marriage in name only.

Jesus desires our faithfulness, not merely our faith. To believe in him is not the same as being faithful to him. He requires a committed love—the *hesed* ("loyal") love described in the Old Testament.

It's time to cast aside would-be lovers and return to the most faithful of partners, God himself, unveiled to us in the person of Jesus Christ.

True love awaits.

❦ PERSONAL RESPONSE

Perhaps we all need a better understanding of the amazing love of God. Maybe then we will realize that no lover can ever replace or duplicate such a love, and we will cease our wandering. Are you ready to turn a blind eye to other suitors?

❦ DIALOGUE WITH GOD

Dear Jesus, I confess that at times I live a parallel life with you. It's not your doing. I wander in and out of your presence like a teenager looking for the car keys or some extra lunch money. Help me to rediscover my first love and to persevere in faithfulness, not just faith. I want to learn to love you again, like I did the first time we met. It is you I seek, and no other.

❦ FURTHER BIBLE READING

John 15

THE LOVER WHO RESPECTS OUR INDIVIDUALITY

Come, follow me, and I will make you fishers of men.

Yesterday's news recounted the case of a woman who had committed identity theft for the last ten years. Using stolen credit card information and social security numbers, she plundered her way through the financial assets of many unsuspecting victims. Each person experienced the same reaction: "I feel violated!" Someone had broken in where she did not belong, had breached barriers that were supposed to be safe. And great damage resulted.

In unhealthy relationships, people "break in" where they do not belong. Some lose their sense of self and violate the space of others, not respecting boundaries. Others withdraw from friends and spouses in times of conflict or uncertainty, failing to bond appropriately. These two components—boundaries and bonding—must co-exist for relationships to thrive. "Bonding is the ability to establish an emotional attachment to another person," writes clinical psychologist Henry Cloud. Boundaries, on the other hand, distinguish us—our thoughts, feelings, emotions, beliefs—from others. Healthy relationships are characterized by appropriate bonding and well-respected boundaries. Unfortunately, our lives are filled with unhealthy relationships.

Watching Jesus deal with people in healthy ways is refreshing. He can express deep love and passion for someone without becoming manipulative, controlling or intrusive. He could mildly rebuke Martha for succumbing to distractions that kept her from a deeper relationship with him and yet still express compassion to her at the death of her brother Lazarus (John 11:5). He could spend all day with his followers without making them feel guilty for taking up so much of his time. The Bible never records Jesus saying, "Look, I've been teach-

ing and healing all day. Can't you people see that I'm tired? Don't you
have any respect for my needs? It sure would be nice to have a little
sleep and some solitude for a change, but I guess that's just too much
to ask, isn't it?"

Though Jesus regularly preached to large audiences he connected
deeply with individuals. Whether encountering the tax collector Zacchaeus in a crowd or meeting a Samaritan woman at a lonely well at
midday, Jesus engaged with each person uniquely and truthfully. But
that shouldn't surprise us—that's what relentless lovers do. Love is
the highest virtue, and love requires that bonding be real and boundaries be honored. Remember how Jesus said, "I stand at the door and
knock"? Note that he didn't say, "Either you open it or I'll bust it
down!" Neither does he manipulate us with comments like, "You
know, if you had any decency you'd let me in. It's cold enough out
here to give even the healthiest rabbi the flu. If I get sick it's on your
conscience!"

Jesus invites without manipulating; he calls without controlling;
he challenges without coercing. He wants us conformed to his image
but not cloned. We are not reproductions of the original with a signature at the bottom of the print. We are unique creations, original
artwork. And Jesus treats us just that way.

Early in my experience as a follower of Jesus, I met a group of people who claimed to know and follow him. But I began to notice
something about them. They dressed the same way, spoke the same
lingo, cut their hair the same style, read the same literature and kept
the same schedules. You would expect some of this in any organiza-
tion, like the military or in a hospital, for example. There are certain
expectations of uniformity and conformity. But these people were not
interested in commonness—they wanted sameness. The leader
wanted everyone to be just like him, and the more you looked like

him, the better you fit in. It was almost cultlike. *Is this what God wants?* I thought. *Replicas of this man, marching off the assembly line like mechanical soldiers?* It was a clear case of personality identity theft.

Like you, I have unique gifts, characteristics and experiences. I was amazed—and remain grateful—that Christ did not ask me to abandon them when I began my relationship with him. Instead, he has asked me to put them at his disposal for use in line with his purposes. I have changed, yes. I am a new creature in Christ, but I am still who God made me to be. I have a different heart, intentions, attitude and focus. Christ has given me new gifts and led me into fresh experiences along the way. He is shining light where there was once only darkness, and he is helping me confront destructive patterns and behaviors. But in all this he is a true lover, respecting how God has made me, taking joy in the fact that I am Bill Donahue, not secretly wishing I was someone else.

Jesus changed Simon's name to Peter and he nicknamed James and John "Sons of Thunder," but he did not change the core of their original design. Each was unique and given a personality that brought God joy and gave the world some diversity. Despite his new relationship to Jesus, Peter remained bold and idealistic, redirecting his efforts toward preaching to crowds and leading the original emerging church. James and John put their fishing skills to work catching people for the kingdom of God. Their skills, talents and experiences were redirected, refocused, reclaimed for kingdom purposes. And you and I do the same, though it does not always mean a change of vocation.

We do not become robotlike followers of Jesus when we experience his grace. He respects our identity—the one he gave us—even as he transforms (not clones) us so that we may joyfully live the abundant life he intended.

Jesus discloses our new identity, the one rooted in our deepening relationship with him (see Ephesians 1). But as he makes us new, he respects our individuality, our distinctiveness. There's only one of us—and he intended it to be that way.

So don't fret about Jesus robbing you of your personality when he promises to change you. Never concern yourself that he will come muscling his way into your life, forcing his agenda on you, expecting you to put on the uniform and march to the same tune as everyone else.

There is no need to fear identity theft—especially from Jesus.

❀ PERSONAL RESPONSE

Reflect on a time when you were expected to become exactly like others to be accepted by them. How did that feel? How did it impact the way you enter relationships today? Are bonding and boundary-setting easy or difficult for you?

❀ DIALOGUE WITH GOD

Lord, I'm grateful for who I am and how you created me. I'm relieved that I don't have to change the core of that wonderful creation to be used by you. There are special and unique aspects of me that I like—and I know you like them too. I also know there are changes in store for me, that you will make me a different person as I move toward you in relationship and growth. My character and heart need work—lots of it. Thank you for not expecting me to be a clone of someone else. As I seek to draw closer, use me. Empower my gifts. Show me how I can be used according to your purposes. I am willing and open to this new life you talk about.

❀ FURTHER BIBLE READING

Ephesians 1

THE LOVER WHO PROTECTS OUR VULNERABILITY

I will not leave you as orphans; I will come to you.

"Love doesn't sound so dangerous until you've tried it." I remember reading that statement and thinking, *Here's someone who gets it.* All true love is dangerous, risky and fragile. "Safe love" is a contradiction in terms. Love requires that we sacrifice personal agendas, redesign personal schedules and recognize personal faults. Suddenly, loving feels vulnerable. Our motives are exposed and our weaknesses magnified as we enter the loving presence of another. Vulnerability is the price we pay for intimacy. It leaves us dangerously unguarded.

Before the fall of communism I had the chance to venture behind the iron curtain. I was traveling with a few others who were volunteering to help a new church in Graz, Austria, and we took a side trip into Bratislava, Czechoslovakia. The boat ride was beautiful and the scenery spectacular—until we turned a corner and crossed into communist territory. On each side of the river stood a watchtower guarded by soldiers with AK-47s. As we passed I turned to look back. Warning signs marked the crossing, intended to deter Czechs from unlawful travel (or escape). For those who lived behind the curtain, this was the danger zone. Everyone who traveled here placed themselves at the mercy of those guards.

I was a relatively new Christian at the time, still finding my way, still seeking answers to many questions. As I stepped from the boat I felt a sense of intense vulnerability. The place was unfamiliar and the language unknown. Though I was probably in no real danger, I was uncomfortable. We were not allowed to take pictures of military personnel or to visit certain areas of the city.

In a Russian bookstore off the main square in Bratislava, a man about forty years old began speaking to the three of us. He did not turn to look directly at us. "You are Americans," he said in clear English.

"Yes, we are. Hello."

He continued, "I am a professor of mathematics at the university here."

After a few cordial exchanges I mentioned we were with a Christian group serving in Austria. After checking over his shoulder he made brief eye contact and spoke in a hushed tone. "If I simply entered a church building here, I would never be able to teach at the university again." He fidgeted as we talked a bit more and then, obviously uncomfortable, he moved on.

In that moment I felt a deep sadness. We all did. We wanted to take him back with us, back to the freedom of Austria and away from this oppressive place that was sucking the joy and life from everyone. I realized just how vulnerable he had been by merely speaking with us, knowing we were involved in something religious. He risked trusting us, momentarily placing himself in our hands, hoping we would not blurt out a foolish remark or somehow compromise his government-sponsored employment. He took a risk because he wanted us to know the weight of oppression he lived with. He wanted his story told. He wanted to be more than just another cog in the Soviet machinery. He wanted to be human. But that meant exposure, trusting we would protect him in this unguarded moment.

Vulnerability is most acute when we place ourselves wholly in the hands of another. This high-risk venture requires yielding control and relinquishing command to another. Military personnel experience vulnerability on the battlefield when their assumptions and actions rely on intelligence reports they trust are accurate. Brave souls venture out into open fields or scamper along war-torn city streets hoping that comrades provide cover during treacherous periods of exposure in the danger zone.

Getting out of bed one morning in 1999 I suddenly felt light-headed and assumed I'd sat up too fast. When it persisted I thought perhaps it was a bit of flu. I decided to go to work and, if things worsened, come home or see a doctor. I never made it that far. After two minutes in my car the symptoms worsened and my heart began beating rapidly. I tried to take a pulse and was shocked to feel it erratic and fluttering. I headed to the emergency room of a nearby hospital and was wired up to a number of monitors. Calmly, the physician on duty informed me I had arrhythmia, an irregular heartbeat.

There I lay, connected to machines and surrounded by bright lights and busy nurses. I knew none of these people and they had never seen me. But they were checking my vital signs and making decisions about my health and my life. It was a vulnerable moment. And there wasn't much I could do about it. The nervousness increased as I pondered horror stories of hospital foul-ups and the incompetence of some workers. *Did the doctor say "cartilage" or "cardiac" medication? Oh well, let's just flip a coin.* But here, as expected, each professional attended to his or her duty, and a quiet trust began to emerge in my spirit. These people knew what they were doing and I was going to be okay.

"When Jesus calls a man, he bids him come and die," said Dietrich Bonhoeffer. Die to self-interest and self-promotion, and place our life wholly in the trusting hands of Christ. It makes no sense intellectually, and it's a precarious and vulnerable posture. But I know it's the right thing to do. I might indeed die, like Bonhoeffer, who chose the vulnerable security of Jesus rather than the seemingly safe hands of people. He knew Jesus would protect that vulnerability. He might not protect him from the evil of the Nazis, but he would protect—cover—his vulnerability. He would never leave him exposed.

When we become vulnerable before God we open our lives to his

gracious work. We become agents of transformation, used according
to his purposes. Bonhoeffer placed himself at the disposal of God,
and it landed him in prison. A theology professor and pastor, he was
changed from being a scholar with many answers to a man with
many questions.

Who am I? This or the other?
Am I both at the same time? In public, a hypocrite
And by myself, a contemptible, whining weakling? . . .
Who I really am, you know me, I am thine, O God.

To be vulnerable before God is to surrender to his guidance and
his will. To give ourselves to his competent and loving care. Only
then are we fully alive and protected—from pretense and temptation
and selfish ambition. We may at first feel alone but we soon experience his resounding presence as his Spirit breathes life into our brokenness. Peace sweeps over us like a warm breeze on a spring afternoon as he whispers words of comfort and hope. In our moment of
greatest vulnerability there is security and soul-rest.

All this I have spoken while still with you. But the Counselor,
the Holy Spirit, whom the Father will send in my name, will
teach you all things and will remind you of everything I have
said to you. Peace I leave with you; my peace I give you. I do
not give to you as the world gives. Do not let your hearts be
troubled and do not be afraid. (John 14:25-27)

Vulnerability is never comfortable. It's simply a prerequisite to
peace. Give your heart, soul, dreams, fears, ambivalence, grief, success and everything else that shields you from God—give it to one
who can handle it. When you enter the danger zone, you will find
Jesus there.

❧ PERSONAL RESPONSE

Reflect for a moment—in what area of your spiritual life do you feel most vulnerable? Why? Are you guarding that area from God?

❧ DIALOGUE WITH GOD

Dear Jesus, I admit that words like weakness, vulnerability, brokenness and surrender are foreign to me, at least in practice. I prefer safety, control and low-risk investment. But I know that real life does not abide there. Give me the courage to lay aside the protective gear I am wearing that shields me from your relentless love. Help me to make friends with vulnerability. And when I do, protect me from myself and fill me with your Spirit.

❧ FURTHER BIBLE READING

John 16:5-24

THE LOVER WHO RELEASES OUR JOY

*I have told you this so that my joy may be in you
and that your joy may be complete.*

Craig Wilson, a reporter for *USA Today*, was in the habit of taking his neighbors' car to the inspection station each year. "It's a little gift I give them, one of those 'random acts of kindness,' if you speak bumper sticker," quips Wilson. On one particular morning at 6:55 a.m., he entered lane four and waited. Soon he was greeted by the inspection attendant. "How are you doing this morning?" the attendant asked.

"Fine," said Wilson. "And you?"

"Blessed," he said. "Blessed."

The response startled Wilson, who remarks, "There he was, dealing with more-than-likely unhappy people, standing outside on a steamy July morning, and he felt blessed. I can't get the man out of my mind." Wilson goes on to ponder why the people who have the worst jobs often appear to be happiest. Like the woman who cleaned the bathrooms at his Washington, D.C., office or the non-English-speaking men who painted his house over the summer, singing and laughing under the hot sun. Finally, Wilson is prompted to ask, "And why is it the people with the most seem the most unhappy?" He remembers an altercation involving a senator's wife whose car was blocking another customer at a garden center. Charges and lawsuits were filed. Wilson's advice? "The judge should have just ordered them all to get their cars inspected. Lane Four." I agree.

Wilson admits he has lots of questions and few answers. But I like his questions. Why do those who have the most seem the most unhappy? Why is it that the most joyous people I've met were a group of struggling South Africans whose employment was questionable and whose futures less than promising?

"I bring you good news of great joy that will be for all the people," promised an angel regarding the birth of Jesus (Luke 2:10). Interestingly, the message was given to people working one of the worst jobs of the day—shepherding.

> *Wanted: Shepherds to care for dumb, smelly sheep. Long hours, low pay, late nights. Regular threats from wolves and robbers. Travel a must. Housing provided (any spot on the ground you can find), health benefits included (the fresh air will do you good). Call 1-800-SHEAR-ME or visit our website: www.bedouin-now-than-never.com.*

Ever wonder why the news was delivered to the shepherds? Like Wilson I have more questions than answers, but perhaps they understood joy. The religious elite would have been nervous, the politically powerful threatened and the wealthy just too busy to notice. Few people were joyful people in Jesus' day, and the trend continues unabated.

John the Baptizer is another example. John was rough and rugged, chiseled by sandstorms in the day and sleeping under the cold stars at night. Yet listen to John:

> You yourselves can testify that I said, "I am not the Christ but am sent ahead of him." The bride belongs to the bridegroom. The friend who attends the bridegroom waits and listens for him, and is full of joy when he hears the bridegroom's voice. That joy is mine, and it is now complete. He must become greater; I must become less. (John 3:28-30)

John in his humility recognized Jesus for who he is and, upon doing so, became elated.

When the disciples realized Jesus was leaving them, sadness filled their souls. But Jesus told them, "Now is your time of grief, but I will see you again and you will rejoice, and no one will take away your joy" (John 16:22).

See a pattern? Here's a final clue. David, prophetically looking forward to the coming of the Christ, said, "You have made known to me the path of life; / you will fill me with joy in your presence" (Psalm 16:11).

Joy is not a feeling; it's a relationship. Jesus wants us to be joyful, and he longs to help us release that joy. But his plan is not a self-help book or a weight-loss strategy or a support group. His plan is a person—Jesus.

When I think of my wife, deep joy fills me. After seventeen years of marriage I would still choose her in a heartbeat. But like all marriages ours has had (and will have) its challenges, disappointments, trials and heartaches. We do not always feel happy—but we have joy. And that joy is released when we have time together: walking, talking, eating at a favorite restaurant or lounging in the family room with a cup of coffee and a movie. It's a relationship. I am her beloved and she is mine.

Joy is found in intimacy and friendship with Jesus, that most relentless of lovers who pursues us with passion and determination. No one can snatch us out of his hand (John 10:28). Joy comes when we recognize that we are his bride, his beloved. We are the objects of his tireless, sacrificial, unconditional, relentless love.

So enjoy the company of Jesus today. He longs to unleash his joy in you. "Until now you have not asked for anything in my name. Ask and you will receive, and your joy will be complete" (John 16:24). Not partial, not temporary, not momentary: complete joy.

And my guess is that when someone asks, "How are you today?" you'll answer, "Blessed!"

PERSONAL RESPONSE

If your relationship with Jesus is distant, irregular or nonexistent, take a moment to understand why. And right now, no matter how you feel, seek his presence. Ask him to spend a few moments with you. Read his words, reflect on his life—and discover joy.

DIALOGUE WITH GOD

Jesus, I'm so grateful that you deliver on your promises. If there's anything I need more of right now, it's joy. So here I am. I want to see you for who you are, love you for what you've done and follow you wherever you lead. Show me your joy that mine might be complete. Thanks, Jesus. I love you.

FURTHER BIBLE READING

Philippians 1:1-26

Jesus

THE SUPREME CONQUEROR

Winning a battle is complex. It requires a plan, and a dozen contingency plans, because plans are useless after the first shot has been fired. Battles quickly become chaotic. You expect the unexpected. The best-trained, best-equipped fighters have an advantage because they are prepared to fight in a variety of circumstances and conditions. And if they are backed up with adequate supply channels and resources, they can sustain the fighting until the battle is won. In some cases, the fight becomes so intense that warriors must call on every resource at their disposal to survive. Few know this better than U.S. Air Force Captain Scott O'Grady.

In 1995 during the crisis in Bosnia, O'Grady's F-16 was struck by a surface-to-air missile, forcing him to eject four miles above enemy territory. Serbian soldiers saw his parachute descend and hunted for him. He dropped into the bush and covered his white ears with dark gloves, lying silent for five hours as hostile forces scoured the area, firing at anything that moved and once walking within a few feet of him.

He spent the next six days in a cat-and-mouse chase, fearful of using his handheld radio to contact U.S. forces since Serbs would be monitoring the airwaves. Using a sponge to soak up water from the rocks and eating bugs and grass, O'Grady put his survival training to work. He had two survival kits, one from the cockpit and the other in his vest, that contained first-aid materials, signal flares, strobe lights, a whistle, a one-man raft, a knife, water, matches, a blanket, a sea dye marker, a pistol, a tourniquet, a radio beacon, camouflage paint, a GPS unit and a handheld radio.

On the sixth day, when O'Grady was suffering from exhaustion, hunger and hypothermia, a search team flying overhead established radio contact with the young pilot. U.S. forces immediately organized a surprise dawn raid—after daylight, helicopters would be sitting ducks for another missile attack. Forty-one Marines piled into two Sea Stallion helicopters, accompanied by two Sea Cobra gunships and four Sea Harrier jets. Other vessels in the area supplied radar-jamming planes, AWAC aircraft to track progress and direct traffic, and several F-18As, F-16s and F-15Es to fly cover and attack threatening ground forces. According to *Newsweek*, it took six billion dollars of equipment and weaponry to rescue one pilot, including forty aircraft, forty-one Marines, three naval vessels and a plethora of state-of-the-art surveillance and radar technology. Every resource available was mobilized.

"How did they not see you?" asked an incredulous reporter after his rescue. O'Grady, who had spent much of the six days praying as he evaded his would-be captors, answered, "God. Period dot."

Our spiritual battle is not unlike O'Grady's ordeal. Yet we are often unaware of the stakes involved or the enemy with whom we contend. Many of us are ignorant of the weapons at our disposal, the arsenal of support we may draw from in times of crisis and when faced with evil. O'Grady was courageous, well-trained and had two survival kits, but he needed the power of an entire military to rescue him.

Our resources are limited, our power lacking and our resolve sporadic. If we intend to survive spiritually in the battle of life, we must call upon the divine resources at our disposal. Behind us stands no mere military force but the power that created the cosmos and governs our world. Our commander holds the universe in his hands and has already secured the victory. There are skirmishes to fight, but the war is won and victory is ours.

Jesus' resources are limitless, his power overwhelming and his resolve unwavering. He confronts the enemy without flinching and offers his strength and guidance as we wage war against the evil that plans our destruction. Our task is to stay the course and fight courageously, utilizing the power and resources provided by our supreme conqueror, Jesus.

Let us prepare for battle.

THE CONQUEROR WHO CONFRONTS OUR ENEMY

Get behind me, Satan!

The street I grew up on in northeast Philadelphia was lined with row homes, narrow two-story dwellings attached to the adjacent houses. Each house had three bedrooms, a one-car garage (in 1964 almost everyone on my street had one car), a small basement and a modest backyard bordered by a chainlink fence. Our home was in the middle of the block, keeping us in the center of any action that occurred. It was a good place to grow up, and I have fond memories of my first nine years of life there.

Like many middle-class neighborhoods near the city limits, ours consisted of young families trying to carve out a respectable life while working at least one job (most of the time my dad had three). There were no seminars on how to raise your kids, and Dr. Phil and Oprah were just kids themselves. "Successful" parenting for many families meant getting their kids through school while keeping them out of jail. Others did their best to give their kids a stable home life and dreamt of a day when they could move to the suburbs to nicer homes, better jobs and more effective schools.

Crime rates were relatively low but we had our share of thugs and bullies—and therefore no shortage of scuffles and fights. When I was six years old there were about five guys my age, a couple who were younger, five eight-year-olds and a couple guys in junior high school.

One of those junior high guys was Michael, and he had everything you look for in a bully. He was older and bigger, insecure, and taunted mercilessly by his older sisters. He seemed to derive great joy from pestering others.

From time to time Michael would shove us around, call us names and commit other acts that kept him off most people's Christmas gift list. One day the roughness intensified and a real threat emerged—I was going to get clobbered. I was alone and had aimlessly wandered toward his end of the block. Generally I tried to fight my own battles, but I knew in this case my opponent was more than I could handle. He caught me and grabbed my sleeve as I scampered for home. A wave of terror washed over me. Michael was going to rearrange my facial features, and I began to scream.

To my surprise and Michael's horror, a screen door smacked open and out popped a fourteen-year-old athletic guy named John. He bounded down the steps and headed straight for Michael. John was bigger, stronger and faster than my adversary, and suddenly the predator became the prey. In a nanosecond Michael let go of me and fled for the safety of his home. My disposition changed from sheer terror to pure joy as he ran screaming up the steps to his front door, which was locked. Time seemed to stand still as the blood drained from Michael's face. Someone must have wanted to protect him from destruction that day, because just as John came within reach the door opened and Michael burst inside, panting like a fox that had barely outrun the hounds. John shouted something I could not hear, but I'm certain Michael did. He never came near me again.

John had a reputation on the block that Michael had either forgotten or never known. Several years earlier, when he was about eight, John was accosted by a group of older boys on the street. There were five of them, and they wanted to fight him. He didn't back down, but he did set some ground rules. "I'll fight you," he said, "but if it's going to be fair, you'll have to fight me one at a time."

They agreed, and John proceeded to defeat each one. The last one, as I recall, didn't stick around to be the final victim. Watching his buddies flee with watering eyes and bloody lips was enough. After that, no one challenged John.

It's great when someone's there to help you confront your worst enemy.

It's great when that someone is bigger, stronger and wiser than you.

And it's really great when that someone is your older brother. Thanks, John!

There are enemies far more destructive and dangerous than the Michaels of the world—enemies that plague our conscience, exploit our weaknesses and take advantage of our vulnerability to sin. Confronting them is always challenging, often overwhelming and sometimes terrifying. These are the battles that ravage the soul and have the potential to corrupt even the most sincere among us. The mastermind behind them, the evil one, takes pleasure in waging this war.

But just as there are enemies far more deadly than Michael ever pretended to be, there is one whose strength and power are far greater than any older brother could ever muster. This one is Jesus. He is fearless when confronting the enemy, and those who trust in him take comfort knowing that his intervention protects the godly and sends the evil one running for cover every time.

"In this world you will have trouble" (John 16:33). Yes, Jesus, you can say that again. Trouble is as certain as death and taxes. "But take heart! I have overcome the world." Now that's the best news I've heard all day.

☙ PERSONAL RESPONSE

Take a moment to identify your greatest enemies, the people or situations that seem to confront you at every turn. Are you willing to call out to Jesus for strength to battle these foes? What will it take for you to trust that he can confront the evil that faces you—even if in the moment it appears that you're losing the battle?

☙ DIALOGUE WITH GOD

God, I'm not much of a warrior. Often I either deny I'm in a battle or retreat from the conflict. Maybe that's because I think I'm facing the enemy alone. Please take this prideful attitude from me and let me call out to you, my rescuer, to vanquish the evil forces that threaten my soul, seeking to weaken my trust in you. I need you to step in and unleash the power I cannot rally to fight a battle I cannot win alone. Thank you for hearing me.

☙ FURTHER BIBLE READING

Ephesians 6:10-20

The Conqueror Who Chooses Our Weapons

This kind can come out only by prayer.

When I traveled to South Africa, we visited Pilanesburg, a beautiful game park about two hours north of Johannesburg. On our rides through the park we were treated to amazing scenery and incredible wildlife encounters, up close and personal. At one point our guide stopped the fifteen-passenger vehicle to quietly observe a group of rhinoceros, including a baby, in the brush about twenty-five feet away. One adult rhinoceros soon began to pace anxiously, its tail pointing in the air.

"What's he doing?" we asked.

"That he is probably a she," the guide clarified. "And though she has trouble seeing us, she's heard us and detected our scent. Let's move along a little." Our guide remained calm and started the engine, slowly moving us to a safer distance. "When a rhino walks with her tail moving about, she feels threatened. It's best not to stay close by when that happens."

"What would happen if she attacked?" I asked, sliding inconspicuously across the seat to the far side of truck.

"It's not likely as long as we remain in the vehicle, but it's best to give them their space," our guide said. I agreed that space was good. Nice rhino. "The rhino thinks we're a large animal. But if someone leaves the truck and she identifies them as a small creature, the likelihood of attack increases. So you'll want to stay in the vehicle."

"But what if a rhino *did* attack?" I pressed, worried that if she charged we'd be the lead story on the evening news. *Stupid Americans anger rhino—details at 11.*

"She probably wouldn't be able to turn this large truck over, but she could smash it around a bit," the guide said matter-of-factly. "Of course, the others might join in and then we'd be in real trouble."

Hmmm. "So there's nothing we could do?"

He pointed to the dashboard and answered, "This is an elephant gun, so we're okay."

Great, but this was a rhino. Didn't we need a rhino gun? Discerning my thoughts, the driver added, "One shot from an elephant gun will kill anything in the park. Any other rifle or handgun would basically just irritate the animal, so having one of these around is nice." He patted the gun like it was his pet Doberman. "Don't worry, we have the right weapon here."

Wow. One shot. My confidence soared and my pulse slowed down a few beats. One shot could take out a two-thousand-pound rhino or an elephant three times that size. I felt better. I felt secure. I felt safe—until I asked another question. "Have you ever had to use it?"

"No," he answered. "I just assume it will do the job when I need it."

"One final question," I ventured politely. "Are you a good shooter?"

He just laughed and said, "Oh look, there are impala off to the left."

My body started turning left but my eyes were glued to the right, on the agitated rhino—just in case she didn't like laughing park rangers. But not to worry; we had the right weapon.

Having the right weapons to fight an impending battle makes all the difference. Ancient Israel feared the Philistines, who had iron shields and spears—major technological advances over their enemies. Early in World War II small and ill-equipped American tanks encountered much larger, heavily armed German Panzers and Tiger tanks. It was a serious mismatch with dire consequences for the Allied forces. The Zulu tribe of South Africa attained a sound advantage over their enemies by designing a short, versatile weapon that they could handle as both a sword and spear. In the time it took opponents to raise their longer, more cumbersome spears above their heads, Shaka Zulu's warriors could quickly strike a deathblow. In each case, superior and effective weapons led to victory in battle.

In Jesus' day his disciples encountered a man possessed by a demon, but they couldn't cast it out. Jesus, frustrated by their inability to practice what he had modeled and taught, explained their failure. "This kind can come out only by prayer" (Mark 9:29). Whatever the disciples had used to fight the spiritual battle confronting them, prayer hadn't been their weapon of choice. Jesus knew what weapons to use.

When he encountered Satan in the wilderness Jesus responded to the evil one's sinister attacks by quoting the Hebrew Scripture he'd studied and loved, beginning each response with "It is written . . ." (see Luke 4:1-13). The Word of God was his weapon of choice in this battle. In other instances Jesus' own rebuke secured victory over evil, showing his followers that his words and the Father's words had equal power and force.

As the kingdom of God expands, encounters with evil are inevitable. These spiritual battles take place in a realm beyond the physical, though the results are often displayed in ways we can see and touch. Paul reminds the church of this reality in the book of Ephesians, where he describes a variety of God-given weapons and defense strategies at the disposal of his followers.

> For our struggle is not against flesh and blood, but against the rulers, against the authorities, against the powers of this dark world and against the spiritual forces of evil in the heavenly realms. Therefore put on the full armor of God, so that when the day of evil comes, you may be able to stand your ground, and after you have done everything, to stand. (Ephesians 6:12-13)

Some of us either ignore the weapons supplied to us or deny the reality of battle, blind to the assault being mounted against us. A friend of mine on staff at Willow Creek has experienced several recent family challenges—surgery for a son, health problems with his wife and now a tumor in his own body. "In some ways this doesn't surprise us," he remarked. "Each time this has happened, it took place during the week we had scheduled a key meeting for an intensive church-wide outreach into the community. But we are praying and we are not backing down from what God has called us to do." He knows he's in a battle and he's using the kingdom weapons at his disposal—prayer, trust in others in his community of faith and reliance on a powerful and loving God.

Partnership with God provides a strategic advantage. New weapons are made available to us to meet the changing demands of the battle that rages. As our relationship with God deepens and we understand the nature of the spiritual realm, we learn to choose our weapons wisely. In the most intense battles, we find we must exhaust the entire arsenal—prayer, community, the wisdom of others who have been in the battle, God's Spirit, the truth found in the Bible and the courage to exercise our faith in Jesus. As Paul says, "And after you have done everything . . ."

For new seekers of God's ways and truths, encountering Jesus as conqueror may feel awkward. The whole military metaphor may disturb you. Jesus, who said, "Blessed are the peacemakers," looks strange in uniform carrying a weapon of any kind. But the life Jesus calls us to will create conflict. When love confronts hate, grace meets legalism and truth dispels lies, conflict is unavoidable. We have encountered Jesus as friend, forgiver, healer and lover, but he is a warrior as well. The raging battle for the soul is an unseen conflict. But it is real, and there are casualties.

Whether you are a curious seeker or convinced follower, I am asking you to enter more fully into the Jesus way of life, a new way of being in the world. But I cannot deceive you. Not everyone will leap with joy as you pursue his ways. It may change the way people relate and respond to you. Forces of darkness are at work, manifesting themselves in oppressive organizations and hurtful people. But God is also at work, revealing himself through loving people and life-giving groups who in his power wage war using the instruments of grace and truth.

I encounter the living Jesus each time I stand and utilize his weapons instead of my own. This decision has proven effective in times of illness, fear, financial challenge and personal loss. The power of God flows freely to those who seek it in ways that honor his purposes. Sometimes he provides a dramatic display, as when a couple on the verge of divorce see their entire demeanor change in a moment. Or when God shows up in a hospital room, bringing comfort, hope and healing. But it's often the everyday battles, the skirmishes of life, in which we must utilize the simple weapons God has given.

When I was negotiating the purchase of a home, the owner insisted on being present throughout the inspection process. When I asked why, she stated, "This is my baby, and no one touches my baby without me being there." I could see the storm clouds forming on the relational horizon, and on the day of the inspection they had become a full-blown weather system. I arrived to find her berating the inspector for scratching her gutters with his ladder. The inspector was fuming. "I don't have to stay here and take this," he said to me. "This woman is crazy. You can find another inspector. I've inspected over five hundred homes and have never had anyone talk to me like this!"

The owner also directed her comments squarely at me. "You called this guy, Mr. Bill Donahue, and you'd better make sure he doesn't hurt my baby!" It was a beautiful moment.

There was no time for drawn-out prayer or deep reflection. But I decided to do two things—say a brief prayer and draw on the wisdom of others who had dealt honorably with conflict. "Jesus," I prayed, "guard my character and grant me wisdom. I need you now. Amen." That was it.

I stood my ground, explaining that no one was leaving and that no one came here to hurt anyone or anything. I encouraged them both to calm down, and I felt my own defensive attitude drain away. Immediately, their tone and demeanor changed. I believe God infused peace directly into the conflict. For the next few minutes we each explained our desires and intentions and set up some boundaries for the process. I mediated the interaction between the owner and inspector, clarifying comments and helping them understand each other's opinions, frustrations and viewpoints. In ninety minutes the inspector was on his way, and the owner's "baby" was safe and sound.

No lights or flashes from heaven. No dramatic music in the background. But Christ had conquered the moment. The weapons of wisdom, grace and prayer had prevailed at the onset of a relational battle. We face dozens of situations like this each week, at work, home and play. Jesus is more than capable of handling them if we simply use the resources he has supplied.

So continue the battle. Stand firm. Fear not.

We have the right weapons.

❧ PERSONAL RESPONSE

Do you know that you are in a battle? If so, when was the last time you took an inventory of the spiritual weapons at your disposal? Could it be that you're losing ground because you're fighting without the weapons God has provided?

❧ DIALOGUE WITH GOD

Dear God, I confess I've been blind to the battle around me. Forgive me for living in denial and apathetic ignorance. And help me to pick up the weapons of faith, truth, prayer and your words to stand firm against the evil that seeks to destroy my trust in you. I am inadequate to fight this fight alone. Help me to confront the enemy with courage, using the resources you supply. Help me to persist in the fight when I'm tempted to surrender. The only person I ever want to surrender to is you. Let us stand firm together. In the strength of Jesus I pray this.

❧ FURTHER BIBLE READING

Luke 4

THE CONQUEROR WHO SUPPLIES OUR STRENGTH

I have given you power and authority.

Battle fatigue can wear down an army, so wise commanders rotate frontline fighters to allow the weary to recover and replenish their strength. Spiritual battles are no different. When struggling with repeated temptation, wrestling with addiction or praying fervently for the protection and healing of a loved one, spiritual weariness soon prevails. The soul becomes heavy, the spirit weak, and emotions fray at the edges. We need spiritual refreshment.

I have seen many people come to a point of spiritual exhaustion. A friend's nephew accidentally kills himself playing a prank with a gun. Another labors under an oppressive boss and tries to maintain integrity while performing with excellence. Yet another is recovering from surgery—again. Emotional and physical burdens leave us with battle fatigue. Life wears us down.

Jesus was familiar with this struggle. Sometimes we forget that the flesh-and-blood Christ had limits as we do. "Someone touched me; I know that power has gone out from me," he said at one point (Luke 8:46). The human condition was his condition, and his invincible deity did not negate his vulnerable humanity. He needed food and sleep for physical restoration; he required the regular replenishment of spiritual resources for his demanding work. Jesus was a channel for God's power, not simply a reservoir of limitless spiritual strength and energy.

> The words I say to you are not just my own. Rather, it is the Father, living in me, who is doing his work. (John 14:10)

Jesus developed a pattern of life to ensure that he had strength for the demands of life and ministry. That pattern involved a perpetual cycle of solitude with the Father, community with others and ministry to the world. Solitude, community, ministry. This pattern, described in Luke 6:12-19, reminds us that the Son of God needed to draw from the spiritual well of prayer and intimacy with the Father so that he could guide his followers in community and meet the challenges of ministry.

In solitude we encounter three voices: the voices of self, the evil one and God. Jesus experienced these voices when he fasted forty days in the desert (Matthew 4). He was challenged by his own humanity and the desires of his flesh, confronted by the evil one who sought to tempt him and destroy his ministry, and loved by his Father from whom he drew power and authority. The voice of self will cry out for attention, point to our weaknesses and demand that we gratify the cravings of our flesh. *Don't spend time in prayer. Watch a movie or take a nap instead. After all, it's probably not good for you to fast and pray, especially with the diet you're on. And it probably wouldn't change anything anyway.*

The voice of evil is filled with accusations and shame, causing us to hate ourselves and doubt God. *You think you're spiritual? What about that woman in your small group you said you'd pray for but never did? Or the way you talked to your best friend last night? You'll never change and never be the person God wants you to be. You're a fake, a hypocrite, a sham.* That voice tears us up and weighs us down.

But then there's God's voice. While we are in prayer and quietness his voice breaks through, reminding us that we are his beloved child, a unique and favored son or daughter of the king. His voice silences the verbal abuse of the evil one and overcomes the insecurities and self-doubt that we hear on the tapes playing over and over in our head. His voice prevails.

Then, as we become centered in his love, forgiveness and strength, we have something to give to our community. As Henri Nouwen explains, "Community is not loneliness clinging to loneliness; it is solitude grabbing onto solitude." We come together with others, enjoying table fellowship, experiencing communal prayer, reading Scripture, perhaps singing, laughing and playing together. From solitude and quietness we enter community, where we meet Jesus in and through others, and then we move into the world as a servant.

Solitude, community and ministry. It's the "Jesus pattern" for strength and restoration, the pattern from which he drew power and authority for the challenges of life and the seemingly endless demands of service to others.

I find fresh wisdom and insight from Jesus when I honor that pattern. Solitude allows me to connect with Christ at a personal level, hearing his voice and revealing my need for God. I remember several years ago lying on the floor in a cabin someone had graciously lent me. I had come to write and prepare for teaching, but I found instead that I was intensely tired. The combination of raising young kids, carrying a heavy ministry responsibility and supporting others who were struggling had exhausted my resources.

I sensed Jesus telling me to take a nap. It was odd and not very spiritual-sounding. I had much to do—good, spiritual stuff like prayer and Bible reading. But I admitted that I was tired, so I lay down for thirty minutes. Four hours later I awoke to the sound of a neighbor's lawnmower. Jesus knew what I needed. Sleep. He knew that rest and spiritual renewal go hand in hand. Referring to our hectic lifestyles a friend once remarked that "Americans crave sleep like hungry people crave food." In most cases we don't realize we crave something much deeper: a connection with God, where our real strength lies. But it cannot be found in the busyness and chaos of a fragmented life.

So what does your pattern look like? If it's like most Americans', it's not solitude, community, ministry. Instead it's activity, individualism, misery.

Jesus is eager to supply our strength, but we must avail ourselves of his power, which flows from the Father, is distributed by Jesus and is activated by the Holy Spirit working in those who follow Christ (Matthew 28:18-20; John 14:26; Acts 1:8).

Our primary access to God's strength and power is through quietness alone in prayer and through people—people who listen, pray and come alongside us to offer themselves as servants. That's the Jesus way. In prayer we boldly ask that God will work in and through us, giving us the strength and courage to act in his name. "Until now you have not asked for anything in my name. Ask and you will receive, and your joy will be complete" (John 16:24). And from people we receive the support and hope we need for the long haul. God's grace flows in and through his community.

In Paul's second letter to a young, struggling church in Corinth, he wrote these words:

> When we came into Macedonia, this body of ours had no rest, but we were harassed at every turn—conflicts on the outside, fears within. But God, who comforts the downcast, comforted us by the coming of Titus, and not only by his coming but also by the comfort you had given him. He told us about your longing for me, your deep sorrow, your ardent concern for me, so that my joy was greater than ever. (2 Corinthians 7:5-7)

God sent Paul Titus. Paul and his team were comforted by God through others. They supplied the strength.

When battle fatigue sets in, connect with Jesus and his people. You will find something you might not have been expecting—true rest from a weary battle.

PERSONAL RESPONSE

When was the last time you stepped back from the battle lines for restoration and replenishment? How can you make this a pattern in your life? With whom can you practice the discipline of community, living life together with others?

DIALOGUE WITH GOD

Jesus, if there was ever a time I needed power it is now. I've never felt more overwhelmed by the responsibilities I carry, the demands I must meet, the needs that confront me and the weakness that fills my soul. I'm weary and need soul rest. Grant me the grace and courage to set time aside to be with you—to allow your voice to calm the raging storms that surround me and disturb my spirit. I need you. I need your power working in me through the

Spirit. I can face this battle no more—and I cannot return to it alone. So help me lean into a community of fellow warriors, a band of brothers and sisters who can fight alongside me and carry me when I'm wounded. Be my supply, I pray.

✺ FURTHER BIBLE READING

John 14

THE CONQUEROR WHO SECURES OUR VICTORY

Take heart, for I have overcome the world.

The 1919 Chicago White Sox were underpaid compared to their rivals. Their best players, like Shoeless Joe Jackson, made six thousand dollars while competitors with half the talent made ten thousand. White Sox players were given three dollars a day for expenses while traveling; other teams were paid four dollars. As a result, team members often resented their owner, Charles Comiskey. Nonetheless this low-paid team played well enough to make it to the World Series against the Cincinnati Reds. Fans were optimistic for a victory. But it wouldn't happen. The series was over before it started.

Eight members of the Sox conspired with gamblers to throw the series to the Reds—for eighty thousand dollars in cash to be divided among them. As the games progressed, reporters and fans became suspicious. Pitchers Eddie Cicote and Lefty Williams intentionally hit batters and threw wildly. Cicote threw an easy double-play ball over the head of the second baseman into the outfield. Reds players made easy hits and were walked often. But then the gamblers appeared to balk on their promise to pay, and by the sixth game the Sox decided to play for real, winning easily and forcing the series to a ninth and final game. But threats and pressure proved too much, and Lefty Williams intentionally pitched so poorly in game nine that Cincinnati jumped ahead and was an easy winner. The 1921 trial convicted the players, and the Sox's reputation would be forever tarnished by the scandal.

The series was fixed, the outcome decided. Certain people knew who was going to win before the first ball ever left the pitcher's hand.

It would be nice if we could "fix" certain situations in life. It would be great to know the cancer tests would return negative before we got the scan. It would be wonderful to know that our child was getting a full scholarship to Harvard despite his C's in biology. It would be fantastic to know that our dating partner would marry us and be a loving spouse for fifty-five years of marriage—before the engagement. It would all be great.

The Bible doesn't leave us guessing about the ultimate outcome of the spiritual battles we face. We may lose a few along the way but the text is clear—Jesus has secured the victory. Heaven is sure and death is only fatal, not final.

> When the perishable has been clothed with the imperishable, and the mortal with immortality, then the saying that is written will come true: "Death has been swallowed up in victory."
> "Where, O death, is your victory?
> Where, O death, is your sting?"
> The sting of death is sin, and the power of sin is the law. But thanks be to God! He gives us the victory through our Lord Jesus Christ. (1 Corinthians 15:54-57)

Followers of Jesus can take comfort in that. As you might, I have some apprehensions about dying. But I don't fear death. Jesus has conquered death and sin, and that brings great comfort and relief.

Death has already lost. The game is over.

It's rigged. It's fixed. We already know the outcome. You can bet on it—legally.

❧ PERSONAL RESPONSE

What concerns you when you think of death and dying? How do you feel knowing Jesus has already taken the effects of death away?

❧ DIALOGUE WITH GOD

Jesus, I do fear the process of dying. I wonder if it will be slow and painful or relatively comfortable and quick. The uncertainty is unnerving. I can't control that event. But I take great comfort, even joy, in knowing that evil is defeated and death is dead. The life that takes pleasure in you now will continue in your presence forever. That gives me great relief. Thank you for enduring so much and defeating the enemy at the point of his greatest strength—the grave.

❧ FURTHER BIBLE READING

1 Corinthians 15:35-58

THE CONQUEROR WHO
CELEBRATES OUR TRIUMPH

I saw Satan fall like lightning.

Remember the story in chapter five about that embarrassing loss we experienced in football my junior year in high school? Thankfully, there's more to the tale.

I made a decision that day. After being trounced 53-0, I overheard a teammate ask a fellow senior, "Where are we going to party tonight?"

We had just been humiliated in front of our parents, teachers, classmates and opponents, and he wanted to know where the party was? I was filled with rage but too tired to do anything about it.

Instead I made a decision—I channeled that rage into a commitment to never lose again. In that moment I caught the eye of another junior, my best friend Paul. I could see he had made the same decision. It was the beginning of a new era. Nine months before our senior year started, we determined that it would not be a year of mediocre performances and embarrassing losses.

We weren't the only ones tired of losing. More than forty players showed up for an off-season weight-training and running program that began in February and continued through the summer. At first it was fun, but soon the weeks wore on and spring was upon us. Classmates bounded out of school to enjoy the warm weather with their girlfriends and their cars while we slaved away in a small, sweaty weight room. It was even harder in the summer.

Despite winning every preseason contest, we entered the regular season as the laughingstock of the league, every newspaper predicting the usual last-place finish.

After winning our third straight game by upsetting a league powerhouse, our fans became believers. After eight games we remained undefeated and headed toward an unprecedented league championship. Only one thing stood in our way—the team that trounced us 53-0 the previous year. I wanted to beat these guys more than anyone we'd ever played. It wasn't about revenge; it was about self-respect. This time we would play the Eagles on their home field. The game was scheduled for—you guessed it—senior parents' day.

This time the tables were turned, and with seconds left in the game we scored the winning touchdown. On that cool Friday night in November 1975 the victory was sweet, especially for those of us on defense who harbored vivid memories of last year's debacle. The smallest, most underrated team in the league had experienced a storybook finish to an amazing undefeated season. And this time, instead of mourning with a group of demoralized players, we celebrated in a caravan of buses filled with band members, cheerleaders and other students. The celebration lasted the entire night.

There's nothing like being celebrated when you experience success—in any endeavor. Sharing the victory with others is almost as much fun as experiencing it yourself.

Jesus' apprentices faced an overwhelming battle when he sent them out in pairs on their first real ministry assignment. Talk about underrated. Their challenge was far greater than ours and made our little football game seem like, well, just a little football game. Let's face it; going door to door proclaiming Jesus as Messiah in a Roman-occupied, Judaism-committed culture was a life-and-death encounter with formidable obstacles, not the least of which were the spiritual battles. Jesus had warned them, "Go! I am sending you out like lambs among wolves" (Luke 10:3). *Hey, Bartholomew. Did he say we were the lambs and they were the wolves? Did I hear that right? I wish he'd said, "Go! I am sending you out as lions among gazelles!"*

Jesus encouraged his team to heal the sick and preach the good news of God's kingdom, activities that would invite strong opposition from all sides. And yet they had great success because Jesus supplied them with the power they needed to fight the battles. After the conflict, the thirty-six pairs of emissaries returned for the debriefing.

The seventy-two returned with joy and said, "Lord, even the demons submit to us in your name."

He replied, "I saw Satan fall like lightning from heaven. I have given you authority to trample on snakes and scorpions and to overcome all the power of the enemy; nothing will harm you. However, do not rejoice that the spirits submit to you, but rejoice that your names are written in heaven." (Luke 10:17-20)

I picture Jesus with a smile on his face as he makes the remark about Satan falling from heaven. Like little children bursting into the house to show mom the results of their successful butterfly hunt, his disciples came bounding along, giving each other high-fives and singing victory choruses. I imagine Jesus enjoyed every minute of this, eager to celebrate with them. And he seized the moment to remind them of the ultimate victory they shared: "that your names are written in heaven."

Every time you and I stand firm for truth, help the impoverished, share the redemptive love story of God's grace in Christ and shout back at the evil that invades our lives, we evoke a smile on the face of Jesus. But this is just the beginning, a hint of the real celebration to come. The joy we find here is only a glimpse of the heavenly celebration that awaits every believer in Jesus. And Jesus will be there to celebrate that day with us.

After this I looked and there before me was a great multitude that no one could count, from every nation, tribe, people and language, standing before the throne and in front of the Lamb. They were wearing white robes and were holding palm branches in their hands. And they cried out in a loud voice:

"Salvation belongs to our God,
who sits on the throne,
and to the Lamb." (Revelation 7:9-10)

Blessed are those who are invited to the wedding supper of the Lamb! (Revelation 19:9)

The heavenly celebration is going to be some kind of party! I'm guessing there will be more than a few buses in the motorcade that day and that traffic will be blocked for a few thousand years.

🎵 PERSONAL RESPONSE

Reflect on what it means to share in and celebrate God's victory over sin and death. How can you acknowledge that today? What does it do for you as you ponder the reality that one day there will be an unending celebration in the heavens?

🎵 DIALOGUE WITH GOD

God, I admit that sometimes I feel like we're on the losing side. Sickness, disease, war, famine, unemployment, poverty, abuse and failure run rampant. Not to mention the unfinished homework, dirty laundry, clogged toilets, ailing cars, shriveling bank accounts and unraveling relationships. But I'm grateful for the many victories—an answered prayer, a smiling child, a warm day in November, a spring rain, a letter from a distant friend, a movie with my spouse, a walk in the woods in autumn, a sales call that goes as planned and the chance to sing Christmas songs again this year, even though there will be an empty seat at the table. I do look forward to the day we can celebrate life together, Jesus. Your smile is what I long to see. This gives me courage and hope. Thanks for celebrating my life and cheering me on.

🎵 FURTHER BIBLE READING

Psalm 96

NOTES

Chapter 1: Jesus, the Provocative Teacher

p. 19   The Microsoft titan: Jim Frederick, "Microsoft's $40 Billion Dollar Bet," *Money*, May 2002, p. 66.

p. 22   "Much of the history": Andrew Greeley, "There's No Solving Mystery of Christ," *Chicago Sun-Times*, January 16, 2004, p. 47.

p. 22   "He was nothing like": Don Everts, *Jesus with Dirty Feet* (Downers Grove, Ill.: InterVarsity Press, 1999), pp. 25-28.

p. 23   "To teach is to create": Parker Palmer, *To Know as We Are Known* (San Francisco: HarperSanFrancisco, 1993), p. 88.

p. 35   "While we are alone": Jean Vanier, *Community and Growth* (Mahwah, N.J.: Paulist Press, 1989), p. 26.

p. 41   "Here lies the basic flaw": Mark Buchanan, *Your God Is Too Safe* (Sisters, Ore.: Multnomah Publishers, 2001), p. 66.

p. 46   "In contemporary Christianity": Brennan Manning, *The Signature of Jesus* (Sisters, Ore.: Multnomah Publishers, 1996), p. 17.

Chapter 2: Jesus, Our Sacred Friend

p. 52   Jesus never really was: Brennan Manning, *A Glimpse of Jesus* (San Francisco: HarperSanFrancisco, 2003), p. 57.

p. 57   "Christ's blood was poured out": Stephen P. Adams, "American Missionary Gunned Down," *Christianity Today*, January 2003, p. 26.

p. 57   Experts estimate: Benedict Rogers, "Burma's Almost Forgotten," *Christianity Today*, March 2004, p. 53.

p. 57   "We have to leave": Ibid.

pp. 59-60 "I was heading down a path": Tim Stafford, "A Heaven-Made Activist," *Christianity Today*, January 2004, p. 49.

p. 60   "I love the bride of Christ": Ibid.

p. 66   Riggers pack parachutes: Brenda Benner, "I Will Be Sure—Always," *Texas Air National Guard Magazine,* June 2001, p. 7.

p. 68   "What's going on here?": The editors of *U.S. News & World Report,* May 6, 2002, p. 4.

p. 71   "We protect our wounds": Larry Crabb, *The Safest Place on Earth* (Nashville: Word Publishing, 1999), p. 33.

p. 77   "Girls in my AP English class": Quoted by Hannah Friedman, "When Your Friends Become the Enemy," *Newsweek*, April 19, 2004, p. 16.

Chapter 3: Jesus, the Truthful Revealer

p. 93   If sales of the Left Behind series: David Gates, "The Pop Prophets," *Newsweek,* May 24, 2004, p. 46.

p. 94   Mende Nazer was kidnapped: Lev Grossman, "Reader, My Story Ends with Freedom," *Time,* February 9, 2004, p. 77.

pp. 97-99   "Once I get to college": Derrick Adkins, "What the World Didn't Know About Me," *Newsweek,* May 7, 2001, p. 12.

Chapter 4: Jesus, the Extreme Forgiver

p. 107   *Die wit man:* Nelson Mandela, *Long Walk to Freedom* (Boston: Back Bay Books, 1994), p. 111.

p. 108   "It is not an easy or pleasant task": Ibid., p. 340.

p. 108   "The authorities liked to say": Ibid., p. 392.

p. 108   "I did not see the face": Ibid., p. 334.

pp. 109-10   "I was asked": Ibid., p. 568.

p. 110   "The truth of the matter is": Lewis Smedes, *Forgive and Forget* (New York: Simon & Schuster, 1984), p. 109.

p. 111   "How privileged we are": Quoted by Philip Yancey, "Lessons from Rock Bottom," *Christianity Today,* July 10, 2000, p. 72.

p. 114   "In our struggle with self-hatred": Brennan Manning, *A Glimpse of Jesus* (San Francisco: HarperSanFrancisco, 2003), pp. 86-87.

p. 117   "The truth is": Don Everts, *The Smell of Sin* (Downers Grove, Ill.: InterVarsity Press, 2003), pp. 93, 95.

p. 119   "Tax collectors were the dung": Ken Gire, *Instructive Moments with the Savior* (Grand Rapids: Zondervan, 1992), p. 35.

p. 133   In the A.D. 120s: Ted Olsen, *Christianity and the Celts* (Downers Grove, Ill.: InterVarsity Press, 2003), p. 37.

pp. 134-35 "The cross, in other words": Gilbert Bilezikian, *Community 101* (Grand Rapids: Zondervan, 1993), pp. 34-35.

Chapter 5: Jesus, the Authentic Leader

p. 139   "An eloquent advocate": Jon Meacham, "American Deamer," *Newsweek,* June 14, 2004, p. 29.

pp. 139-40 "There is some solace": Patti Davis, "The Gemstones of Our Years," *Newsweek,* June 2004, p. 43.

p. 141   "We all have fears": Faith Hopler and Erika Larson, "Searching for the Real Thing," *Relevant,* July-August 2004, pp. 31-32.

p. 144   "There are many paths": Guy Spiro, "Many Paths to One," *The Monthly Aspectarian,* November 2003, p. 13.

p. 150   "Exploration brings surprise": Paul Cody, "Mission Modified," *Outdoor Explorer,* February-March 2001, p. 104.

p. 155   "Sin is the unwillingness": Quoted by Richard Kauffman, "Sin and Evil," *Christianity Today,* October 2004, p. 100.

Chapter 6: Jesus, the Compassionate Healer

p. 179   "Community life brings a painful revelation": Jean Vanier, *Community and Growth* (Mahwah, N.J.: Paulist Press, 1989), pp. 26-27.

pp. 180-81 "The very last thought": Gilbert Bilezikian, *Christianity 101* (Grand Rapids: Zondervan, 1993), p. 185.

Chapter 7: Jesus, Our Relentless Lover

p. 185   "Here, then, is the full account": Dallas Willard, *Renovation of the Heart* (Colorado Springs: NavPress, 2002), p. 132.

p. 188   Liesel Pritzker is ten times richer: Nara Schoenberg, "Billion-dollar baby," *Chicago Tribune,* March 25, 2005, section 5, pp. 3-4.

p. 189   "Our love for God": Scot McKnight, *The Jesus Creed* (Brewster, Mass.: Paraclete, 2004), pp. 42-43.

p. 190   Psychology professor Elizabeth Paul: Daniel McGinn, "Mating Behavior 101," *Newsweek,* October 4, 2004, pp. 44-45.

p. 191   Over the last ten years: Lorraine Ali and Lisa Miller, "The Secret Lives of Wives," *Newsweek,* July 12, 2004, pp. 46-54.

p. 191   "Couples begin to live": Ibid., p. 51.

p. 193   "Bonding is the ability": Henry Cloud, *Changes That Heal* (Grand Rapids:

Zondervan, 1990), p. 46.

p. 197   "Love doesn't sound": Paul Wadell, quoted in McKnight, *Jesus Creed,* p. 54.

p. 200   "Who am I?": Dietrich Bonhoeffer, quoted by Dave Fleming, "Leadership Wisdom from Unlikely Voices," *Rev. Magazine,* September-October 2004, p. 116.

p. 201   "It's a little gift": Craig Wilson, "How Many Can Pass the 'I'm Blessed' Inspection Test?" *USA Today,* July 28, 2004, p. 1.

Chapter 8: Jesus, the Supreme Conqueror

p. 205   "O'Grady's F-16 was struck": Evan Thomas, "An American Hero," *Newsweek,* June 19, 1995, pp. 24-33.

If you want more resources to help people connect to Jesus and to one another in community life in your church, go to <www.willowcreek.com> and check the Small Group Resources portion of the website. If you would like to contact Bill Donahue directly for questions or feedback, or to create additional learning experiences using In the Company of Jesus, *e-mail him at bdonahue@willowcreek.org, and we will do our best to serve you.*